THE **100** MOST IMPORTANT BIBLE VERSES FOR DEALING WITH YOUR EMOTIONS

SMITH
FREEMAN
Publishing

TABLE OF CONTENTS BY TOPIC

A MESSAGE TO READERS

Emotions: we relish the good ones and dread the bad ones. Given the choice, we would spend all our days feeling joyful, grateful, peaceful, and happy. But life doesn't always work that way. Sometimes we're attacked by negative emotions that darken our thoughts and harden our hearts.

The Lord wants you to guard your heart against negative emotions and destructive behaviors. So He has given you a guidebook for spiritual, emotional, physical, and psychological health. That book, of course, is the Holy Bible. The Bible is a priceless gift, an infallible tool that God intends for you to use every day, in good times and in hard times. Your intentions should be the same.

This book contains one hundred essential Bible verses that are intended to help you deal with your emotions—and the emotions of others—while staying faithful to the teachings contained in God's holy Word. If you sometimes feel like you're on an emotional roller coaster, or if you're plagued by negative emotions that leave you feeling angry, disheartened, or hopeless, the ideas on these pages will provide the wisdom, the courage, and the practical advice you'll need for managing your thoughts and improving your outlook.

When you weave God's message into the fabric of your day—and into the realities of your everyday relationships—you'll quickly discover that God's Word has the power to change everything, including your attitude and your responses. So, if you sincerely desire to find better strategies for dealing with the emotional ups and downs of everyday life, don't give up. Instead, keep searching for direction: God's direction. When you do, you'll discover the comfort, the power, the wisdom, and the peace that only He can give.

Seven Essential Steps for Dealing with Your Emotions

Accept the fact that chronic negative emotions can be dangerous to your mental, spiritual, and physical health. God wants you to experience the abundant life that He describes in John 10:10. To achieve it, you must guard your heart against negative emotions and the destructive behaviors that negative emotions inevitably cause.

Understand that it's possible to manage your emotions. If you believe that you have no control over your emotions, you're wrong. It may take training, education, and practice, but if you sincerely desire to gain better control over your emotions, you can do it. With God, all things are possible.

Identify any chronic negative feelings and turn them over to God. Make no room in your heart for anger, regret, bitterness, envy, or any other negative emotion that threatens your sanity and steals your joy. When you feel these emotions begin to invade your thoughts, interrupt the process with a silent prayer.

Understand that emotions are highly contagious. Unless you make the conscious effort to take control of your thoughts and emotions, other people's emotional outbursts can hijack yours. If you find yourself in a situation where another person's negative emotions are continually infecting yours, ask God to help you guard your heart. And while you're at it, establish as much physical and psychological distance as you can by establishing clear boundaries between yourself and the difficult person.

Forgive everybody. Hate and peace cannot coexist in the same human heart. So the sooner you forgive everybody—including yourself—the sooner you'll begin feeling better about yourself and your world.

When you experience a significant loss, express your feelings honestly. If you're experiencing tough times or recovering from a tragic loss, don't keep everything bottled up inside. Express your grief. And while you're at it, remember that God promises to heal the brokenhearted. In time, He will dry your tears if you let Him. If you haven't already allowed Him to begin His healing process, today is a perfect day to start.

If your emotions—or the emotions of someone you love—begin to spiral out of control, seek professional help immediately. Small emotional swings are an inevitable part of everyday life. But dramatic emotional swings—either extreme, unrelenting sadness or manic symptoms such as grandiose thinking or intense irritability—are dangerous. So don't be embarrassed to seek professional help. Mental health professionals have numerous tools at their disposal to help you deal with emotional swings and mood disorders. Since help is available, you should ask for it as soon as you detect a problem.

1

ANGER

LEARN TO CONTROL ANGER BEFORE IT CONTROLS YOU

Everyone must be quick to hear, slow to speak, and slow to anger, for man's anger does not accomplish God's righteousness.
JAMES 1:19–20 HCSB

Anger is a natural human emotion that is sometimes necessary and appropriate. Even Jesus became angry when confronted with the moneychangers in the temple: "And Jesus entered the temple and drove out all those who were buying and selling in the temple, and overturned the tables of the moneychangers and the seats of those who were selling doves" (Matthew 21:12 NASB).

Righteous indignation is an appropriate response to evil, but God does not intend that anger should rule our lives. Far from it. God intends that we turn away from anger whenever possible and forgive our neighbors just as we seek forgiveness for ourselves.

Life is full of frustrations, some great and some small. On occasion, you, like Jesus, will confront evil, and when you do, you may respond as He did: vigorously and without reservation. But more often your frustrations will be of the more mundane variety. As long as you live here on earth, you will face countless opportunities to lose your temper over small, relatively insignificant events: a traffic jam, a spilled cup of coffee, an inconsiderate comment, or a broken promise. When you are tempted to lose your temper over the minor inconveniences of life, don't. Turn away from anger, hatred, bitterness, and regret. Turn instead to God. When you do, you'll be following His commandments and giving yourself a priceless gift: the gift of peace.

More Thoughts about Anger

Life is too short to spend it being angry, bored, or dull.
BARBARA JOHNSON

Anger and bitterness—whatever the cause—
only end up hurting us. Turn that anger over to Christ.
BILLY GRAHAM

Frustration is not the will of God. There is time
to do anything and everything that God wants us to do.
ELISABETH ELLIOT

Hence it is not enough to deal with the temper.
We must go to the source, and change the inmost nature,
and the angry humors will die away of themselves.
HENRY DRUMMOND

Hot heads and cold hearts never solved anything.
BILLY GRAHAM

More from God's Word

Do not let the sun go down on your anger,
and do not give the devil an opportunity.
Ephesians 4:26–27 NASB

He who is slow to wrath has great understanding,
but he who is impulsive exalts folly.
Proverbs 14:29 NKJV

But now you must also put away all the following: anger,
wrath, malice, slander, and filthy language from your mouth.
Colossians 3:8 HCSB

A hot-tempered man stirs up conflict,
but a man slow to anger calms strife.
Proverbs 15:18 HCSB

But I tell you that anyone who is angry
with his brother is subject to judgment.
Matthew 5:22 NIV

A Timely Tip

Don't be caught up in another person's emotional outbursts. Emotions are highly contagious, and angry encounters almost never have happy endings. So if someone is ranting, raving, or worse, give yourself permission to leave the scene of the argument.

2

ANXIETY

MANAGING ANXIETY

Cast all your anxiety on him because he cares for you.
1 PETER 5:7 NIV

Ours is an anxious generation. We live in an uncertain world, a world where tragedies can befall the most righteous (and the most innocent) among us. Yet even on those difficult days when our anxieties threaten to overwhelm us, we can be assured that God stands ready to protect us. Psalm 147 promises, "He heals the brokenhearted and bandages their wounds" (v. 3 NCV). So when we are troubled or anxious, we must call upon the Lord, and, in His own time and according to His own plan, He will heal us.

Sometimes our anxieties may stem from physical causes: chemical reactions in the brain that produce severe emotional distress or crippling panic attacks. In such cases, modern medicine offers hope to those who suffer. But oftentimes our anxieties result from spiritual deficits, not physical ones. And when we're spiritually depleted, the best prescription is found not in the medicine cabinet but deep inside the human heart. What we need is a higher daily dose of God's love, God's peace, God's assurance, and God's presence. And how do we acquire these blessings from our Creator? Through prayer, through meditation, through worship, and through trust.

Prayer is a powerful antidote to anxiety; so too is a regular time of devotional reading and meditation. When we spend quiet moments in the divine presence of our heavenly Father, we are reminded once again that our troubles are temporary but His love is not.

As you face the inevitable challenges of everyday living, do you find yourself becoming anxious, troubled, discouraged, or fearful? If so, turn every one of your concerns over to your heavenly Father. The same God who created the universe will comfort you if you ask Him. Your job, simply put, is to ask Him.

MORE THOUGHTS ABOUT ANXIETY

So often we pray and then fret anxiously, waiting for God to hurry up and do something. All the while God is waiting for us to calm down, so He can do something through us.
CORRIE TEN BOOM

Some people feel guilty about their anxieties and regard them as a defect of faith, but they are afflictions, not sins. Like all afflictions, they are, if we can so take them, our share in the passion of Christ.
C. S. LEWIS

He treats us as sons, and all He asks in return is that we shall treat Him as a Father whom we can trust without anxiety. We must take the son's place of dependence and trust, and we must let Him keep the father's place of care and responsibility.
HANNAH WHITALL SMITH

More from God's Word

Therefore do not worry about tomorrow,
for tomorrow will worry about its own things.
Sufficient for the day is its own trouble.
MATTHEW 6:34 NKJV

Peace I leave with you; My peace I give to you;
not as the world gives do I give to you. Do not let
your heart be troubled, nor let it be fearful.
JOHN 14:27 NASB

Let not your heart be troubled;
you believe in God, believe also in Me.
JOHN 14:1 NKJV

Do not be anxious about anything, but in everything,
by prayer and petition, with thanksgiving,
present your requests to God.
PHILIPPIANS 4:6 NIV

Cast your burden on the LORD, and He shall sustain you;
He shall never permit the righteous to be moved.
PSALM 55:22 NKJV

A Timely Tip

If anxious feelings become debilitating or if you're unable to sleep because of racing thoughts or irrational worries, consult your physician. Your anxiety may have physical causes that are contributing to your distress. Help is available. Ask for it.

3

ARGUMENTS

AVOIDING DEAD-END ARGUMENTS

Avoiding a fight is a mark of honor;
only fools insist on quarreling.
PROVERBS 20:3 NLT

Time and again, God's Word warns us against angry outbursts and needless arguments. Arguments are seldom won but often lost, so when we acquire the unfortunate habit of habitual bickering, we do harm to our friends, to our families, to our coworkers, and to ourselves. When we engage in petty squabbles, our losses usually outpace our gains.

If you're dealing with a difficult person, you may be tempted to "take the bait" and argue over matters great and small. If you find yourself in that predicament, take a deep breath, say a silent prayer, and calm yourself down. Arguments are a monumental waste of time and energy. And since you're unlikely to win the argument anyway, there's no rational reason to participate.

Your words have echoes that extend beyond the here and now. So avoid anguished outpourings. Suppress your impulsive outbursts. Curb the need to criticize. Terminate tantrums. Learn to speak words that lift others up as you share a message of encouragement and hope with a world that needs both. When you talk, choose the very same words that you would use if Jesus were listening to your every word. Because He is.

MORE THOUGHTS ABOUT ARGUMENTS

An argument seldom convinces anyone
contrary to his inclinations.
THOMAS FULLER

Argument is the worst sort of conversation.
JONATHAN SWIFT

Most serious conflicts evolve from
our attempts to control others
who will not accept our control.
WILLIAM GLASSER

Never persist in trying to set people right.
HANNAH WHITALL SMITH

Whatever you do when conflicts arise, be wise.
Fight against jumping to quick conclusions
and seeing only your side. There are always
two sides on the streets of conflict. Look both ways.
CHARLES SWINDOLL

More from God's Word

People with quick tempers cause trouble,
but those who control their tempers stop a quarrel.
PROVERBS 15:18 NCV

If any man among you seem to be religious, and bridleth not his
tongue, but deceiveth his own heart, this man's religion is vain.
JAMES 1:26 KJV

A soft answer turneth away wrath:
but grievous words stir up anger.
PROVERBS 15:1 KJV

I tell you that on the day of judgment
people will have to account for every careless
word they speak. For by your words you will be acquitted,
and by your words you will be condemned.
MATTHEW 12:36–37 HCSB

Do everything without grumbling and arguing,
so that you may be blameless and pure.
PHILIPPIANS 2:14–15 HCSB

A Timely Tip

Arguments usually cause many more problems than they solve. And if you're dealing with a highly emotional person, you probably won't win the argument anyway. So don't be afraid to leave the scene of an argument rather than engage in a debate that cannot be won.

4

ASKING GOD FOR HELP

ASK GOD FOR HELP
TO CONTROL YOUR EMOTIONS

Ask, and it shall be given to you; seek, and you shall find;
knock, and it shall be opened to you. For everyone
who asks receives, and he who seeks finds,
and to him who knocks it will be opened.
MATTHEW 7:7–8 NASB

If you're dealing with roller-coaster emotions, you need God's help. And if you ask Him, He will most certainly provide the help you need. So, how often do you ask the Lord for His help and His wisdom? Occasionally? Intermittently? Whenever you experience a crisis? I hope you've acquired the habit of asking for God's assistance early and often. And hopefully you have learned to seek His guidance in every aspect of your life.

Jesus made it clear to His disciples: they should petition God to meet their needs. So should you. Genuine, heartfelt prayer produces powerful changes in you and in your world. God can do great things through you if you have the courage to ask Him (and the determination to keep asking Him). But don't expect Him to do all the work. When you do your part, He will do His part—and when

He does, you can expect miracles to happen.

The Bible promises that God will guide you if you let Him. Your job is to let Him. But sometimes you will be tempted to do otherwise. Sometimes you'll be tempted to go along with the crowd, even when the crowd is heading in the wrong direction. Other times you'll be tempted to do things your way, not God's way. When you feel those temptations, resist them. Instead, ask the Lord to lead you, to protect you, and to correct you. Then trust the answers He gives.

God stands at the door and waits. When you knock, He opens. When you ask, He answers. Your task, of course, is to make God a full partner in every aspect of your life—and to seek His guidance prayerfully, confidently, and often.

ASKING GOD FOR THE THINGS YOU NEED

God will help us become the people we are meant to be, if only we will ask Him.
HANNAH WHITALL SMITH

It's important that you keep asking God to show you what He wants you to do. If you don't ask, you won't know.
STORMIE OMARTIAN

We honor God by asking for great things when they are a part of His promise. We dishonor Him and cheat ourselves when we ask for molehills where He has promised mountains.
VANCE HAVNER

More from God's Word

*You did not choose me, but I chose you and appointed you
so that you might go and bear fruit—fruit that will last—
and so that whatever you ask in my name the Father will give you.*
JOHN 15:16 NIV

*Do not be anxious about anything,
but in everything, by prayer and petition,
with thanksgiving, present your requests to God.*
PHILIPPIANS 4:6 NIV

*Your Father knows the things
you have need of before you ask Him.*
MATTHEW 6:8 NKJV

*The effective prayer of a righteous man
can accomplish much.*
JAMES 5:16 NASB

*Until now you have asked for nothing in My name.
Ask and you will receive, that your joy may be complete.*
JOHN 16:24 HCSB

A Timely Tip

If you're having trouble dealing with your emotions, ask for God's help. And remember that if you have questions, God has answers. So when in doubt, pray. And keep praying until the answers arrive.

5

ATTITUDE

MAINTAIN THE RIGHT KIND OF ATTITUDE

You must have the same attitude that Christ Jesus had.
PHILIPPIANS 2:5 NLT

Attitudes are the mental filters through which we view and interpret the world around us. Positive attitudes produce positive emotions; negative attitudes don't.

The quality of your attitude will help determine the quality of your life, so you must guard your thoughts accordingly. If you make up your mind to approach life with a healthy mixture of realism and optimism, you'll be rewarded. But if you allow yourself to fall into the unfortunate habit of negative thinking, you will doom yourself to unhappiness or mediocrity or worse.

So the next time you find yourself dwelling upon the negative aspects of your life, refocus your attention on things positive. The next time you find yourself falling prey to the blight of pessimism, stop yourself and turn your thoughts around. The next time you're tempted to waste valuable time gossiping or complaining, or revisiting past misfortunes, resist those temptations. Count your blessings instead of your hardships. And thank the Giver of all things good for gifts that are simply too numerous to count.

More Thoughts about Attitude

Your attitude, not your aptitude,
will determine your altitude.
ZIG ZIGLAR

We choose what attitudes we have right now.
And it's a continuing choice.
JOHN MAXWELL

Developing a positive attitude means
working continually to find
what is uplifting and encouraging.
BARBARA JOHNSON

The things we think are the things that feed our souls.
If we think on pure and lovely things,
we shall grow pure and lovely like them;
and the converse is equally true.
HANNAH WHITALL SMITH

The longer I live the more convinced I become
that life is 10 percent what happens to us
and 90 percent how we respond to it.
CHARLES SWINDOLL

Each of us makes his own weather.
FULTON J. SHEEN

More from God's Word

This is the day the LORD has made;
let us rejoice and be glad in it.
PSALM 118:24 HCSB

A merry heart makes a cheerful countenance.
PROVERBS 15:13 NKJV

Rejoice always; pray without ceasing.
1 THESSALONIANS 5:16–17 NASB

Be glad and rejoice, because your reward is great in heaven.
MATTHEW 5:12 HCSB

Finally, brothers, rejoice. Become mature,
be encouraged, be of the same mind, be at peace,
and the God of love and peace will be with you.
2 CORINTHIANS 13:11 HCSB

A Timely Tip

As a Christian, you have every reason on earth—and in heaven—to have a positive attitude. After all, God is in charge; He loves you; and He's prepared a place for you to live eternally with Him. To improve your attitude, focus more intently on the Lord's blessings. Today and every day, try to focus your thoughts on the positive aspects of life, not the negative ones. It is through gratitude, not grumpiness, that you will claim the best that life has to offer.

6

BITTERNESS

BEWARE OF BITTERNESS

Let all bitterness, wrath, anger, clamor,
and evil speaking be put away from you, with all malice.
And be kind to one another, tenderhearted,
forgiving one another, even as God in Christ forgave you.
EPHESIANS 4:31–32 NKJV

Bitterness is spiritual sickness. It will consume your soul; it is dangerous to your emotional health; it can destroy you if you let it. Your task, simply put, is to destroy bitterness before it destroys you.

The world holds few if any rewards for those who remain angrily focused upon the unchangeable past or upon the shortcomings of others. Still, the act of forgiveness is difficult for all but the most saintly men and women. Being frail, fallible, imperfect human beings, most of us are quick to anger, quick to blame, slow to forgive, and even slower to forget. Yet we know that it's best to forgive others, just as we, too, have been forgiven.

If you are caught up in intense feelings of anger or resentment, you know all too well the destructive power of these emotions. How can you rid yourself of these feelings? First, you must prayerfully ask God to cleanse your heart. Then, you must learn to catch yourself whenever angry thoughts begin to invade your consciousness. You must learn to resist those negative thoughts before they hijack your emotions. When you learn to direct your thoughts toward more positive topics, you'll be protected from the spiritual and emotional consequences of bitterness. And you'll be wiser, healthier, and happier too.

MORE THOUGHTS ABOUT THE DANGERS OF BITTERNESS

Bitterness sentences you to relive the hurt over and over.
LEE STROBEL

Bitterness imprisons life; love releases it.
HARRY EMERSON FOSDICK

Bitterness is anger gone sour, an attitude of deep discontent that poisons our souls and destroys our peace.
BILLY GRAHAM

Bitterness is a spiritual cancer, a rapidly growing malignancy that can consume your life. Bitterness cannot be ignored but must be healed at the very core, and only Christ can heal bitterness.
BETH MOORE

Life appears to me too short to be spent in nursing animosity or registering wrong.
CHARLOTTE BRONTË

More from God's Word

Do not judge, and you will not be judged.
Do not condemn, and you will not be condemned.
Forgive, and you will be forgiven.
Luke 6:37 HCSB

The heart knows its own bitterness,
and a stranger does not share its joy.
Proverbs 14:10 NKJV

But when you are praying, first forgive anyone
you are holding a grudge against, so that your
Father in heaven will forgive your sins, too.
Mark 11:25 NLT

Do all things without complaining
and disputing, that you may become
blameless and harmless, children of God
without fault in the midst of a crooked
and perverse generation, among whom
you shine as lights in the world.
Philippians 2:14–15 NKJV

A Timely Tip

The Bible warns that bitterness is both dangerous and self-destructive. So today, make a list of the people you need to forgive and the things you need to forget. Then ask God to give you the strength to forgive and move on.

7

BLAME

DON'T PLAY THE BLAME GAME

But each person should examine his own work,
and then he will have a reason for boasting
in himself alone, and not in respect to someone else.
For each person will have to carry his own load.
GALATIANS 6:4–5 HCSB

To blame others for our own problems is the height of futility, yet casting blame upon others is a favorite human pastime. Why? Because blaming is much easier than fixing, and criticizing others is much easier than improving ourselves. So instead of solving our problems legitimately (by doing the work required to solve them), we are inclined to pass the buck while doing precious little else. When we do, our problems, quite predictably, remain unsolved.

You've probably heard people refer to "the blame game." But in truth, spending inordinate amounts of time blaming others is not a game at all. It is, instead, a self-destructive behavior that impedes our progress, limits our opportunities, and makes us unhappy.

Have you acquired the bad habit of blaming others for problems that you could or should solve yourself? If so, you are wasting time and energy. So instead of looking for someone to blame, look for something to fix, and then get busy fixing it. And as you consider your own situation, remember this: God has a way of helping those who help themselves, but He doesn't spend much time helping those who don't.

More Thoughts about Blaming Others

You'll never win the blame game,
so why even bother to play?
Marie T. Freeman

Do not think of the faults of others
but what is good in them and faulty in yourself.
St. Teresa of Ávila

Make no excuses. Rationalize nothing.
Blame no one. Humble yourself.
Beth Moore

Man must cease attributing his problems
to his environment, and learn again to exercise
his will—his personal responsibility
in the realm of faith and morals.
Albert Schweitzer

Bear with the faults of others as you
would have them bear with yours.
Phillips Brooks

More from God's Word

Don't let your spirit rush to be angry,
for anger abides in the heart of fools.
Ecclesiastes 7:9 HCSB

All bitterness, anger and wrath, shouting and slander must
be removed from you, along with all malice.
And be kind and compassionate to one another,
forgiving one another, just as God also forgave you in Christ.
Ephesians 4:31–32 HCSB

Therefore, laying aside falsehood, speak truth each one of you
with his neighbor, for we are members of one another.
Ephesians 4:25 NASB

The heart knows its own bitterness,
and a stranger does not share its joy.
Proverbs 14:10 NKJV

People's own foolishness ruins their lives,
but in their minds they blame the Lord.
Proverbs 19:3 NCV

A Timely Tip

Blame focuses your mind on the negative aspects of your life. So learn to count your blessings, not your misfortunes. And while you're at it, remember that you can't ever win the blame game, so don't play.

8

BURNOUT

AVOIDING BURNOUT

But those who wait on the LORD shall renew their strength;
they shall mount up with wings like eagles, they shall run
and not be weary, they shall walk and not faint.
ISAIAH 40:31 NKJV

Has the busy pace of life robbed you of the peace that might otherwise be yours through Jesus Christ? If so, you are simply too busy for your own good, and you're in danger of burning out.

Through His only begotten Son, God offers you a peace that passes human understanding, but He won't force His peace upon you. In order to experience it, you must slow down long enough to sense His presence and His love.

Time is a nonrenewable gift from above. How will you use it? You know from experience that you should invest some time each day in yourself, but finding time to do so is easier said than done. As a busy citizen of the twenty-first century, you may have difficulty investing large blocks of time in much-needed thought and self-reflection. If so, it may be time to reorder your priorities.

If you don't prioritize your day, other people will. Before you know it, you'll be taking on lots of new commitments, doing many things but doing few things well. God, on the other hand, encourages you to slow down, to quiet yourself, and to spend time with Him. And you can be sure that God's way is best.

How will you organize your life? Will you carve out quiet moments with the Creator? And while you're at it, will you focus your energies and your resources on only the most important tasks on your to-do list? Will you summon the strength to say no when it's appropriate, or will you max out your schedule, leaving much of your most important work undone?

Today, slow yourself down, commit more time to God, and spend less time on low-priority tasks. When you do, you'll be amazed at how the Father can revolutionize your life.

MORE THOUGHTS ABOUT AVOIDING BURNOUT

There are many burned-out people who think more is always better, who deem it unspiritual to say no.
SARAH YOUNG

Beware of having so much to do that you really do nothing at all because you do not wait upon God to do it aright.
C. H. SPURGEON

Drop the idea that you are Atlas carrying the world on your shoulders. The world would go on without you. Don't take yourself too seriously.
NORMAN VINCENT PEALE

MORE FROM GOD'S WORD

Careful planning puts you ahead in the long run;
hurry and scurry puts you further behind.
PROVERBS 21:5 MSG

Abundant peace belongs to those who love Your instruction;
nothing makes them stumble.
PSALM 119:165 HCSB

But godliness with contentment is a great gain.
1 TIMOTHY 6:6 HCSB

Don't burn out; keep yourselves fueled and aflame.
Be alert servants of the Master, cheerfully expectant.
Don't quit in hard times; pray all the harder.
ROMANS 12:11–12 MSG

I leave you peace; my peace I give you. I do not give it to you
as the world does. So don't let your hearts be troubled or afraid.
JOHN 14:27 NCV

A TIMELY TIP

God can make all things new, including you. If you're feeling burned out or emotionally distraught, slow down, say a silent prayer, and focus on God's promises. And while you're at it, remember that Lord can renew your spirit and restore your strength. Your job, of course, is to let Him.

9

CELEBRATION

THE TIME TO CELEBRATE IS NOW

Rejoice always, pray without ceasing, in everything give thanks;
for this is the will of God in Christ Jesus for you.
1 THESSALONIANS 5:16–18 NKJV

Today is a nonrenewable resource: once it's gone, it's gone forever. Our responsibility, as thoughtful believers, is to use this day in the service of God's will and in the service of His people. When we do so, we enrich our own lives and the lives of those whom we love.

God has richly blessed us, and He wants you to rejoice in His gifts. That's why this day—and each day that follows—should be a time of prayer and celebration as we consider the Good News of God's free gift: the gift of eternal life through Jesus Christ.

Oswald Chambers correctly observed, "Joy is the great note all throughout the Bible." E. Stanley Jones echoed that thought when he wrote, "Christ and joy go together." But even the most dedicated believers can, on occasion, forget to celebrate each day for what it is: a priceless gift from God.

What do you expect from the day ahead? Are you expecting the Lord to do wonderful things, or are you living beneath a cloud of apprehension and doubt? Today, celebrate the life that God has given you. Today, put a smile on your face, kind words on your lips, and a song in your heart. Be generous with your praise and free with your encouragement. And then, when you have celebrated life to the full, invite your friends to do likewise. After all, this is God's day, and He has given us clear instructions for its use. We are commanded to rejoice and be glad. So, with no further ado, let the celebration begin...

MORE THOUGHTS ABOUT CELEBRATING LIFE

There is not one blade of grass, there is no color in this world that is not intended to make us rejoice.

JOHN CALVIN

The greatest honor you can give Almighty God is to live gladly and joyfully because of the knowledge of His love.

JULIANA OF NORWICH

All our life is celebration to us. We are convinced, in fact, that God is always everywhere.

ST. CLEMENT OF ALEXANDRIA

Every day we live is a priceless gift of God, loaded with possibilities to learn something new, to gain fresh insights.

DALE EVANS ROGERS

*Joy is the direct result of having God's perspective
on our daily lives and the effect of loving our Lord enough
to obey His commands and trust His promises.*

BILL BRIGHT

MORE FROM GOD'S WORD

I came that they may have life, and have it abundantly.
JOHN 10:10 NASB

A happy heart is like a continual feast.
PROVERBS 15:15 NCV

I delight greatly in the LORD; my soul rejoices in my God.
ISAIAH 61:10 NIV

*This is the day which the LORD has made;
let us rejoice and be glad in it.*
PSALM 118:24 NASB

Rejoice in the Lord always. Again I will say, rejoice!
PHILIPPIANS 4:4 NKJV

A TIMELY TIP

When times are tough and your emotions are on edge, it's easy to become discouraged. Easy, but wrong. Even during the darkest days, you still have many reasons to celebrate. So focus on the positive aspects of life and count your blessings, not your hardships. Your blessings are, indeed, too numerous to count, but it never hurts to try.

10

CHEERFULNESS

A CHEERFUL HEART:
IT'S GOOD MEDICINE

A cheerful heart is good medicine,
but a crushed spirit dries up the bones.
PROVERBS 17:22 NIV

Few things in life are more sad, or, for that matter, more absurd, than the sight of grumpy Christians trudging unhappily through life. Christ promises us lives of abundance and joy if we accept His love and His grace. Yet sometimes even the most righteous among us are beset by fits of ill temper and frustration. During these moments, we may not feel like turning our thoughts and prayers to Christ, but that's precisely what we should do.

English clergyman Charles Kingsley observed, "The people whom I have seen succeed best in life have always been cheerful and hopeful people who went about their business with smiles on their faces." And John Wesley noted, "Sour godliness is the devil's religion." These words remind us that pessimism and doubt are some of the most important tools that Satan uses to achieve his objectives. Our challenge, of course, is to ensure that Satan cannot use these tools on us.

Are you a cheerful Christian even when times are tough and people are being difficult? You should be! And what is the best way to attain the joy that is rightfully yours? By giving Christ what is rightfully His: your heart, your soul, and your life.

MORE THOUGHTS ABOUT CHEERFULNESS

It is not fitting, when one is in God's service,
to have a gloomy face or a chilling look.
ST. FRANCIS OF ASSISI

The greatest honor you can give
Almighty God is to live gladly and joyfully
because of the knowledge of His love.
JULIANA OF NORWICH

A life of intimacy with God is characterized by joy.
OSWALD CHAMBERS

The practical effect of Christianity is happiness,
therefore let it be spread abroad everywhere!
C. H. SPURGEON

God is good, and heaven is forever.
And if those two facts don't cheer you up,
nothing will.
MARIE T. FREEMAN

More from God's Word

Do everything without grumbling and arguing,
so that you may be blameless and pure.
PHILIPPIANS 2:14–15 HCSB

Rejoice always, pray without ceasing,
in everything give thanks;
for this is the will of God in Christ Jesus for you.
1 THESSALONIANS 5:16–18 NKJV

Shout for joy to the LORD, all the earth.
Worship the LORD with gladness;
come before him with joyful songs.
PSALM 100:1–2 NIV

This is the day that the LORD has made.
Let us rejoice and be glad today!
PSALM 118:24 NCV

A cheerful heart has a continual feast.
PROVERBS 15:15 HCSB

A Timely Tip

Cheerfulness is its own reward, but not its only reward. When you sow a positive attitude, you'll reap a positive life. That's one reason, but not the only reason, that you should count your blessings and be cheerful today and every day.

11

COMPLAINING

SAY NO TO CHRONIC COMPLAINING

Be hospitable to one another without complaining.
1 PETER 4:9 HCSB

Because we are imperfect human beings, we often lose sight of our blessings. Ironically, most of us have more blessings than we can count, but we may still find reasons to complain about the minor frustrations of everyday life. To do so, of course, is not only wrong; it is also the pinnacle of shortsightedness and a serious roadblock on the path to spiritual abundance.

Sometimes we give voice to our complaints, and on other occasions we manage to keep our protestations to ourselves. But even when no one else hears our complaints, God does.

Would you like to feel more comfortable about your circumstances and your life? Then promise yourself that you'll do whatever it takes to ensure that you focus your thoughts on the major blessings you've received, not the minor hardships—or the difficult people—you must occasionally endure. So the next time you're tempted to complain about the inevitable frustrations of everyday living, don't do it. Today and every day, make it a practice to count your opportunities, not your inconveniences. It's the truly decent way to live.

More Thoughts
about Complaining

*If we have our eyes upon ourselves, our problems,
and our pain, we cannot lift our eyes upward.*
Billy Graham

*Don't complain. The more you complain about things,
the more things you'll have to complain about.*
E. Stanley Jones

*Thanksgiving or complaining—these words express two
contrasting attitudes of the souls of God's children.
The soul that gives thanks can find comfort in everything;
the soul that complains can find comfort in nothing.*
Hannah Whitall Smith

*It is always possible to be thankful for what is given
rather than to complain about what is not given.
One or the other becomes a habit of life.*
Elisabeth Elliot

*Life is too short to nurse one's misery. Hurry across the lowlands
so that you may spend more time on the mountaintops.*
Phillips Brooks

*Grumbling and gratitude are, for the child of God,
in conflict. Be grateful and you won't grumble.
Grumble and you won't be grateful.*
Billy Graham

More from God's Word

My dear brothers and sisters,
always be willing to listen and slow to speak.
JAMES 1:19 NCV

Those who guard their lips preserve their lives,
but those who speak rashly will come to ruin.
PROVERBS 13:3 NIV

Those who consider themselves religious
and yet do not keep a tight rein on their tongues
deceive themselves, and their religion is worthless.
JAMES 1:26 NIV

A fool's displeasure is known at once,
but whoever ignores an insult is sensible.
PROVERBS 12:16 HCSB

Do everything without complaining or arguing.
Then you will be innocent and without any wrong.
PHILIPPIANS 2:14–15 NCV

A Timely Tip

If you feel a personal pity party coming on, slow down and start counting your blessings. If you fill your heart with gratitude, there's simply no room left for complaints.

12

CONFIDENCE

DRAW CONFIDENCE FROM GOD

*Let us hold tightly without wavering to the hope we affirm,
for God can be trusted to keep his promise.*
HEBREWS 10:23 NLT

Are you confident about your future, or do you live under a cloud of uncertainty and doubt? If you trust God's promises, you have every reason to live comfortably and confidently. But despite God's promises, and despite His blessings, you may, from time to time, find yourself being tormented by negative emotions. If so, it's time to redirect your thoughts and your prayers.

Even the most optimistic men and women may be overcome by occasional bouts of fear and doubt. You are no different. But even when you feel discouraged—or worse—you should remember that God is always faithful, and you are always protected.

Every life, including yours, is a series of successes and failures, celebrations and disappointments, joys and sorrows, hopes and doubts. But even when you feel very distant from God, remember that He is never distant from you. When you sincerely seek His presence, He will touch your heart, calm your fears, and restore your confidence. No challenge is too big for Him. Not even yours.

More Thoughts
about Confidence

Never yield to gloomy anticipation.
Place your hope and confidence in God.
He has no record of failure.

LETTIE COWMAN

When a train goes through a tunnel and it gets dark,
you don't throw away your ticket and jump off.
You sit still and trust the engineer.

CORRIE TEN BOOM

One of the marks of spiritual maturity
is the quiet confidence that God is in control,
without the need to understand why He does what He does.

CHARLES SWINDOLL

Faith and obedience are bound up
in the same bundle. He that obeys God, trusts God;
and he that trusts God, obeys God.

C. H. SPURGEON

Confidence imparts a wonderful
inspiration to its possessor.

JOHN MILTON

Never be afraid to trust an unknown future to a known God.

CORRIE TEN BOOM

More from God's Word

For our gospel came not unto you in word only, but also in power, and in the Holy Ghost, and in much assurance.
1 Thessalonians 1:5 KJV

Let us draw near with a true heart in full assurance of faith, our hearts sprinkled clean from an evil conscience and our bodies washed in pure water.
Hebrews 10:22 HCSB

In quietness and in confidence shall be your strength.
Isaiah 30:15 KJV

As for God, his way is perfect: the word of the LORD is tried: he is a buckler to all those that trust in him.
Psalm 18:30 KJV

And this is the secret: Christ lives in you. This gives you assurance of sharing his glory.
Colossians 1:27 NLT

A Timely Tip

If negative emotions have caused you to doubt your abilities or your opportunities, it's time for a complete mental makeover. God created you for a purpose, and He has important work specifically for you. So don't let anyone steal your joy, your self-confidence, or your faith in God.

13

COURAGE

WHEN YOUR HEART IS TROUBLED, HAVE COURAGE

For God has not given us a spirit of fearfulness,
but one of power, love, and sound judgment.
2 TIMOTHY 1:7 HCSB

Every person's life is a tapestry of events: some wonderful, some not-so-wonderful, and some downright disastrous. When we visit the mountaintops of life, praising God isn't hard—in fact, it's easy. In our moments of triumph, we can bow our heads and thank God for our victories. But when we fail to reach the mountaintops, when we endure the inevitable losses that are a part of every person's life, we find it much tougher to give God the praise He deserves. Yet wherever we find ourselves, whether on the mountaintops of life or in life's darkest valleys, we must still offer thanks to God, giving thanks in all circumstances.

God is not a distant being. He is not absent from our world, nor is He absent from your world. God is not "out there"; He is "right here," continuously reshaping His universe, and continuously reshaping the lives of those who dwell in it.

The Lord is with you always, listening to your thoughts and

prayers, watching over your every move. If the demands of everyday life weigh down upon you, you may be tempted to ignore God's presence or—worse yet—to lose faith in His promises. But when you quiet yourself and acknowledge His presence, God will touch your heart and restore your courage.

MORE THOUGHTS ABOUT COURAGE

Action springs not from thought,
but from a readiness for responsibility.
DIETRICH BONHOEFFER

In my experience, God rarely makes our fear disappear.
Instead, He asks us to be strong and take courage.
BRUCE WILKINSON

Courage is not simply one of the virtues,
but the form of every virtue at the testing point.
C. S. LEWIS

Just as courage is faith in good,
so discouragement is faith in evil,
and, while courage opens the door to good,
discouragement opens it to evil.
HANNAH WHITALL SMITH

Do not limit the limitless God! With Him,
face the future unafraid because you are never alone.
LETTIE COWMAN

More from God's Word

Behold, God is my salvation;
I will trust, and not be afraid.
ISAIAH 12:2 KJV

Be on guard.
Stand firm in the faith.
Be courageous. Be strong.
1 CORINTHIANS 16:13 NLT

But He said to them,
"It is I; do not be afraid."
JOHN 6:20 NKJV

I can do all things
through Him who strengthens me.
PHILIPPIANS 4:13 NASB

Be strong and courageous, and do the work.
Do not be afraid or discouraged,
for the LORD God, my God, is with you.
1 CHRONICLES 28:20 NIV

A Timely Tip

It takes insight and courage to deal effectively with negative emotions. If you need insight, talk to people you trust and spend time studying God's Word. And if you need courage, ask the Lord to help you do what needs to be done. Now.

14

COURTESY

BE COURTEOUS,
EVEN WHEN IT'S HARD

Finally, all of you be of one mind,
having compassion for one another;
love as brothers, be tenderhearted, be courteous.
1 PETER 3:8 NKJV

Did Christ instruct us in matters of etiquette and courtesy? Of course He did. Christ's instructions are clear: "In everything, therefore, treat people the same way you want them to treat you, for this is the Law and the Prophets" (Matthew 7:12 NASB). Jesus did not say, "In some things, treat people as you wish to be treated." And He did not say, "From time to time, treat others with kindness." Christ said that we should treat others as we wish to be treated in every aspect of our daily lives. This, of course, is a tall order indeed, but as Christians, we are commanded to do our best.

Today, be a little kinder than necessary to family members, friends, and total strangers. And as you consider all the things that Christ has done in your life, honor Him with your words and with your deeds. He expects no less, and He deserves no less.

More Thoughts about Courtesy

Every time you smile at someone,
it is an action of love,
a gift to that person,
a beautiful thing.
MOTHER TERESA

The glory of the home is hospitality.
HENRY VAN DYKE

Courtesy is contagious.
MARIE T. FREEMAN

Hospitality is threefold:
for one's family, this of necessity;
for strangers, this is courtesy;
for the poor, this is charity.
THOMAS FULLER

The habit of being uniformly
considerate toward others
will bring increased happiness to you.
GRENVILLE KLEISER

A man's manners are a mirror
in which he shows his portrait.
GOETHE

More from God's Word

Do not neglect to show hospitality to strangers,
for by this some have entertained angels without knowing it.
HEBREWS 13:2 NASB

So, my friends, when you come together
to the Lord's Table, be reverent and courteous
with one another.
1 CORINTHIANS 11:33 MSG

Kind words are like honey—
sweet to the soul and healthy for the body.
PROVERBS 16:24 NLT

Do to others as you would have them do to you.
LUKE 6:31 NIV

Let everyone see that you are gentle and kind.
The Lord is coming soon.
PHILIPPIANS 4:5 NCV

A Timely Tip

The Golden Rule always applies, even when people are behaving badly and you're feeling edgy. When you feel an outburst coming on, resist the temptation to fight fire with fire. Instead, be as courteous as you can and keep your temper in check. Remember that anger is only one letter away from danger.

15

DAILY DEVOTIONAL

START EVERY DAY WITH GOD

*Morning by morning he wakens me and opens
my understanding to his will. The Sovereign LORD
has spoken to me, and I have listened.*

ISAIAH 50:4–5 NLT

A great way to prepare yourself for the rigors of everyday living is by spending a few moments with God every morning. Whether you're dealing with roller-coaster emotions or stressful circumstances, you need God as your partner. So if you find that you're simply "too busy" for a daily chat with your Father in heaven, it's time to take a long, hard look at your priorities and your values.

Each day has 1,440 minutes. Do you value your relationship with God enough to spend a few of those minutes with Him? He deserves that much of your time and more. Is He receiving it from you? Hopefully so.

As you consider your plans for the day ahead, here's a tip: Organize your life around this simple principle: "God first." When you place your Creator where He belongs—at the very center of your day and your life—the rest of your priorities will fall into place.

More Thoughts about Your Daily Devotional

Whatever is your best time in the day,
give that to communion with God.
Hudson Taylor

Begin each day with God.
It will change your priorities.
Elizabeth George

The entire day receives order and discipline
when it acquires unity. This unity must be sought
and found in morning prayer.
The morning prayer determines the day.
Dietrich Bonhoeffer

Make it the first morning business
of your life to understand some part
of the Bible clearly, and make it
your daily business to obey it.
John Ruskin

Relying on God has to begin all over again
every day as if nothing had yet been done.
C. S. Lewis

Doesn't God deserve the best minutes of your day?
Billy Graham

More from God's Word

But grow in the grace and knowledge
of our Lord and Savior Jesus Christ.
To Him be the glory both now and to the day of eternity.
2 PETER 3:18 HCSB

Heaven and earth will pass away,
but My words will never pass away.
MATTHEW 24:35 HCSB

Early the next morning, while it was still dark,
Jesus woke and left the house.
He went to a lonely place, where he prayed.
MARK 1:35 NCV

Thy word is a lamp unto my feet,
and a light unto my path.
PSALM 119:105 KJV

It is good to give thanks to the LORD,
and to sing praises to Your name, O Most High.
PSALM 92:1 NKJV

A Timely Tip

A regular time of quiet reflection, prayer, and Bible study will allow you to praise your Creator, to focus your thoughts, and to seek God's guidance on matters great and small. Don't miss this opportunity.

16

DEALING WITH CHANGE

DEALING WITH CONSTANT CHANGE

To every thing there is a season,
and a time to every purpose under the heaven.
ECCLESIASTES 3:1 KJV

Our world is in a state of constant change. God is not. At times the world seems to be trembling beneath our feet. But we can be comforted in the knowledge that our heavenly Father is the rock that cannot be shaken.

Every day that we live, we mortals encounter a multitude of changes—some good, some not so good. And on occasion, all of us must endure life-changing personal losses that leave us heartbroken. When we do, our heavenly Father stands ready to comfort us, to guide us, and—in time—to heal us.

Is the world spinning a little too fast for your liking? Are you facing difficult circumstances or unwelcome changes? If so, please remember that God is far bigger than any problem you may face. So instead of worrying about life's inevitable challenges, put your faith in the Father and His only begotten Son. After all, "Jesus Christ is the same yesterday, today, and forever" (Hebrews 13:8 NKJV). And it is precisely because your Savior does not change that you can face your challenges with courage for today and hope for tomorrow.

Are you anxious about situations that you cannot control? Take your anxieties to God. Are you troubled? Take your troubles to Him. Does your little corner of the universe seem to be trembling beneath your feet? Seek protection from the One who cannot be moved. The same God who created the universe will protect you if you ask Him, so ask Him, and then serve Him with willing hands and a trusting heart.

More Thoughts about Dealing with Change

Are you on the eve of change? Embrace it. Accept it.
Don't resist it. Change is not only a part of life,
change is a necessary part of God's strategy.
To use us to change the world, He alters our assignments.
Max Lucado

Transitions are almost always signs of growth,
but they can bring feelings of loss. To get somewhere new,
we may have to leave somewhere else behind.
Fred Rogers

Change the fabric of your own soul
and your own visions, and you change all.
Vachel Lindsay

Ask the God who made you to keep remaking you.
Norman Vincent Peale

More from God's Word

I am the Lord, and I do not change.
Malachi 3:6 NLT

*But grow in the grace and knowledge
of our Lord and Savior Jesus Christ.
To Him be the glory both now and forever. Amen.*
2 Peter 3:18 NKJV

*Then He who sat on the throne said,
"Behold, I make all things new."*
Revelation 21:5 NKJV

*When I was a child, I spoke like a child,
I thought like a child, I reasoned like a child.
When I became a man, I put aside childish things.*
1 Corinthians 13:11 HCSB

*The wise see danger ahead and avoid it,
but fools keep going and get into trouble.*
Proverbs 22:3 NCV

A Timely Tip

Change is inevitable; growth is not. God will come to your doorstep on countless occasions with opportunities to learn and to grow. And He will knock. Your challenge, of course, is to open the door.

17

DEALING WITH DIFFICULT PEOPLE

WHEN DIFFICULT PEOPLE THREATEN TO HIJACK YOUR EMOTIONS

Bad temper is contagious—don't get infected.
PROVERBS 22:25 MSG

Sometimes people can be cruel, discourteous, untruthful, or rude. When other people do things or say things that are hurtful, you may be tempted to strike back with a verbal salvo of your own. But before you say words that can never be unsaid, slow down, say a quiet prayer, and remember this: God corrects other people's behaviors in His own way, and He doesn't need your help (even if you're totally convinced you're in the right).

The Bible teaches us to be self-controlled, thoughtful, and mature. But the world often tempts us to behave otherwise. Everywhere we turn, or so it seems, we see undisciplined, unruly role models who behave impulsively yet experience few, if any, negative consequences. So it's not surprising that when we meet folks whose personalities conflict with our own, we're tempted to respond in undisciplined, unruly ways. But there's a catch: if we fall prey to immaturity or impulsivity, those behaviors inevitably cause us many more problems than they solve.

So when other people behave cruelly, foolishly, or impulsively, as they will from time to time, don't allow yourself to become caught up in their emotional distress. Instead, speak up for yourself as politely as you can and, if necessary, walk away. Next, forgive everybody as quickly as you can. Then, get on with your life, and leave the rest up to God.

MORE THOUGHTS ABOUT DEALING WITH DIFFICULT PEOPLE

How often should you forgive the other person?
Only as many times as you want God to forgive you!
MARIE T. FREEMAN

Never allow sick attitudes to poison your thinking,
nor let ill will make you ill.
NORMAN VINCENT PEALE

Give me such love for God and men
as will blot out all hatred and bitterness.
DIETRICH BONHOEFFER

If you are having difficulty loving or relating
to an individual, take him to God.
Bother the Lord with this person.
Don't you be bothered with him—
leave him at the throne.
CHARLES SWINDOLL

More from God's Word

Mockers can get a whole town agitated,
but the wise will calm anger.
PROVERBS 29:8 NLT

Stay away from a foolish man;
you will gain no knowledge from his speech.
PROVERBS 14:7 HCSB

Don't make friends with an angry man,
and don't be a companion of a hot-tempered man,
or you will learn his ways and entangle yourself in a snare.
PROVERBS 22:24–25 HCSB

A person with great anger bears the penalty;
if you rescue him, you'll have to do it again.
PROVERBS 19:19 HCSB

A perverse man stirs up conflict,
and a gossip separates close friends.
PROVERBS 16:28 NIV

A Timely Tip

Pick your friends wisely. If you want to maintain a positive attitude, it's important to associate with people who are upbeat, optimistic, and encouraging. Sometimes misguided people may attempt to alleviate their own pain by inflicting pain upon others. If you find yourself on the receiving end of someone else's wrath, give yourself permission to walk away.

18

Dealing with Failure

Experiencing Setbacks and Staying on Course

For though the righteous fall seven times, they rise again.
PROVERBS 24:16 NIV

If you want to be happy, consistently happy, you must learn how to deal with failure. Why? Because all of us face setbacks from time to time. Those occasional disappointments are simply the price we pay for being dues-paying members of the human race.

Hebrews 10:36 advises, "Patient endurance is what you need now, so that you will continue to do God's will. Then you will receive all that he has promised" (NLT). These words remind us that when we persevere, we will eventually receive the rewards that God has promised us. What's required is perseverance, not perfection.

When we face hardships, God stands ready to protect us. Our responsibility, of course, is to ask Him for protection. When we call upon Him in heartfelt prayer, He will answer—in His own time and according to His own plan—and He will do His part to heal us. We, of course, must do our part too. And while we are waiting for God's plans to unfold and for His healing touch to restore us, we can be comforted in the knowledge that our Creator can overcome any obstacle, even if we cannot.

More Thoughts about Experiencing Failure

Mistakes offer the possibility for redemption
and a new start in God's kingdom. No matter what
you're guilty of, God can restore your innocence.
Barbara Johnson

No amount of falls will really undo us
if we keep picking ourselves up after each one.
C. S. Lewis

No matter how badly we have failed,
we can always get up and begin again.
Our God is the God of new beginnings.
Warren Wiersbe

Every calamity is a spur and valuable hint.
Ralph Waldo Emerson

Failure is one of life's most powerful teachers.
How we handle our failures determines
whether we're going to simply "get by" in life or "press on."
Beth Moore

Those who have failed miserably
are often the first to see God's formula for success.
Erwin Lutzer

More from God's Word

Weeping may endure for a night,
but joy cometh in the morning.
PSALM 30:5 KJV

If you listen to correction to improve your life,
you will live among the wise.
PROVERBS 15:31 NCV

But as for you, be strong; don't be discouraged,
for your work has a reward.
2 CHRONICLES 15:7 HCSB

We are hard-pressed on every side,
yet not crushed; we are perplexed, but not in despair.
2 CORINTHIANS 4:8 NKJV

The LORD is near to those who have a broken heart.
PSALM 34:18 NKJV

A Timely Tip

Setbacks are inevitable, but your response to them is optional. You and the Lord, working together, can always find a way to turn a stumbling block into a stepping stone, so don't give up, and never abandon hope. Better days will arrive, and perhaps sooner than you think.

19

DEPRESSION

UNDERSTANDING DEPRESSION

He heals the brokenhearted and binds up their wounds.
PSALM 147:3 HCSB

It has been said, and with good reason, that depression is the common cold of mental illness. Why? Because depression is such a common malady. But make no mistake: depression is a serious condition that, if untreated, can take a terrible toll on individuals and families alike.

The sadness that accompanies any significant loss is an inescapable fact of life. Throughout our lives, all of us must endure the kinds of deep personal losses that leave us struggling to find hope. But in time we move beyond our grief as the sadness runs its course and gradually abates. Depression, on the other hand, is a physical and emotional condition that is, in almost all cases, treatable with medication and counseling. Depression is not a disease to be taken lightly. Left untreated, it poses real danger to a person's physical health and emotional wellbeing.

If you find yourself feeling "blue," perhaps it's a logical reaction to the ups and downs of daily life. But if your feelings of sadness have lasted longer than you think they should—or if someone close to you fears that your sadness may have evolved into clinical depression—it's time to seek professional help.

Here are a few simple guidelines to consider as you make decisions about possible medical treatment:

- If you have persistent urges toward self-destructive behavior, or if you feel as though you have lost the will to live, consult a professional counselor or physician immediately.
- If someone you trust urges you to seek counseling, schedule a session with a professionally trained counselor to evaluate your condition.
- If you experience persistent and prolonged changes in sleep patterns, or if you experience a significant change in weight (either gain or loss), consult your physician.
- If you are plagued by consistent, prolonged, severe feelings of hopelessness, consult a physician, a professional counselor, or your pastor.

In the familiar words of John 10:10, Jesus promises, "I have come that they may have life, and that they may have it more abundantly" (NKJV). And in John 15:11, He states, "These things I have spoken to you, that My joy may remain in you, and that your joy may be full" (NKJV). These two passages make it clear: our Lord intends that we experience lives of joyful abundance through Him. Our duty, as grateful believers, is to do everything we can to receive the joy and abundance that can be ours in Christ—and the term "everything" includes appropriate medical treatment when necessary.

Some days are light and happy, and some days are not. When we face the inevitable dark days of life, we must choose how we will respond. Will we allow ourselves to sink even more deeply into our own sadness, or will we do the difficult work of pulling ourselves out? We bring light to the dark days of life by turning first to God, and then to trusted family members, to friends, and, in some cases, to medical professionals. When we do, the clouds will eventually part, and the sun will shine once more upon our souls.

MORE THOUGHTS ABOUT DEPRESSION

Perhaps the greatest psychological, spiritual, and medical need that all people have is the need for hope.
BILLY GRAHAM

Emotions we have not poured out in the safe hands of God can turn into feelings of hopelessness and depression. God is safe.
BETH MOORE

I am sure it is never sadness—a proper, straight, natural response to loss—that does people harm, but all the other things, all the resentment, dismay, doubt, and self-pity with which it is usually complicated.
C. S. LEWIS

Feelings of uselessness and hopelessness are not from God, but from the evil one, the devil, who wants to discourage you and thwart your effectiveness for the Lord.
BILL BRIGHT

More from God's Word

Your heart must not be troubled.
Believe in God; believe also in Me.
JOHN 14:1 HCSB

When I sit in darkness,
the LORD will be a light to me.
MICAH 7:8 NKJV

Weeping may endure for a night,
but joy cometh in the morning.
PSALM 30:5 KJV

Blessed are the poor in spirit: for theirs
is the kingdom of heaven. Blessed are they that mourn:
for they shall be comforted.
MATTHEW 5:3–4 KJV

Why are you cast down, O my soul?
And why are you disquieted within me?
Hope in God; for I shall yet praise Him,
the help of my countenance and my God.
PSALM 42:11 NKJV

A Timely Tip

If you're feeling very sad or deeply depressed, talk about it with people who can help. Don't hesitate to speak with your doctor or your pastor, or both. Help is available. Ask for it.

20

DIFFICULT CIRCUMSTANCES

TRUST HIM IN EVERY CIRCUMSTANCE

Trust in him at all times, you people,
pour out your hearts to him, for God is our refuge.
PSALM 62:8 NIV

Every human life (including yours) is a tapestry of events: some grand, some not-so-grand, and some downright disheartening. When we reach the mountaintops of life, praising God is easy. But, when the storm clouds form overhead and we find ourselves in the dark valley of despair, our faith is stretched, sometimes to the breaking point. As Christians, we can be comforted: wherever we find ourselves, whether at the top of the mountain or in the depths of the valley, God is there, and because He cares for us, we can live courageously.

The Bible promises this: Tough times are temporary but God's love is not; God's love lasts forever. So what does that mean to you? Just this: from time to time, everybody faces tough times, and so will you. And when tough times arrive, God will always stand ready to protect you and heal you.

Psalm 147 promises, "He heals the brokenhearted (v. 3 NIV), but it doesn't say that He heals them instantly. Usually it takes time (and maybe even a little help from you) for God to fix things. So if you're facing tough times, face them with God by your side. If you find yourself in any kind of trouble, pray about it and ask God for help. And be patient. God will work things out, just as He has promised, but He will do it in His own way and in His own time.

MORE THOUGHTS ABOUT TRUSTING GOD IN DIFFICULT CIRCUMSTANCES

Jesus did not promise to change the circumstances around us. He promised great peace and pure joy to those who would learn to believe that God actually controls all things.
CORRIE TEN BOOM

Accept each day as it comes to you. Do not waste your time and energy wishing for a different set of circumstances.
SARAH YOUNG

Don't let obstacles along the road to eternity shake your confidence in God's promises.
DAVID JEREMIAH

No time is too hard for God, no situation too difficult.
NORMAN VINCENT PEALE

No matter what our circumstance, we can find a reason to be thankful.
DAVID JEREMIAH

More from God's Word

I have learned in whatever state I am, to be content.
PHILIPPIANS 4:11 NKJV

The LORD is a refuge for the oppressed,
a refuge in times of trouble.
PSALM 9:9 HCSB

God is our protection and our strength.
He always helps in times of trouble.
PSALM 46:1 NCV

Cast your burden on the LORD,
and He shall sustain you;
He shall never permit the righteous to be moved.
PSALM 55:22 NKJV

The LORD is a refuge for His people and a stronghold.
JOEL 3:16 NASB

A Timely Tip

No circumstances are too tough for God, and no problems are too big for Him. When times are tough, cast your burden upon Him, and He will sustain you.

21

DIFFICULT RELATIONSHIPS

NAVIGATING DIFFICULT RELATIONSHIPS

It is safer to meet a bear robbed of her cubs
than to confront a fool caught in foolishness.
PROVERBS 17:12 NLT

Emotional health is contagious, and so is emotional distress. If you're fortunate enough to be surrounded by family members and friends who celebrate life and praise God, consider yourself profoundly blessed. But if you find yourself caught in an unhealthy relationship, it's time to look realistically at your situation and begin making changes.

Don't worry about changing other people; you can't do it. What you can do is conduct yourself in a responsible fashion and insist that other people treat you with the dignity and consideration that you deserve.

In a perfect world filled with perfect people, our relationships, too, would be perfect. But none of us are perfect and neither are our relationships...and that's okay. As we work to make our imperfect relationships a little happier and healthier, we grow as individuals and as families. But if we find ourselves in relationships that are debilitating or dangerous, then changes must be made, and soon.

If you find yourself caught up in a personal relationship that is bringing havoc into your life, and if you can't seem to find the courage to do something about it, don't hesitate to consult your pastor. Or you may seek the advice of a trusted friend or a professionally trained counselor. But whatever you do, don't be satisfied with the status quo.

God has grand plans for your life; He has promised you the joy and abundance that can be yours through Him. But to fully experience God's gifts, you need happy, emotionally healthy people to share them with. It's up to you to make sure that you do your part to build the kinds of relationships that will bring abundance to you, to your family, and to God's world.

MORE THOUGHTS ABOUT NAVIGATING DIFFICULT RELATIONSHIPS

Most serious conflicts evolve from our attempts
to control others who will not accept our control.
WILLIAM GLASSER

An argument seldom convinces anyone
contrary to his inclinations.
THOMAS FULLER

When dealing with other people, remember
that you are not dealing with creatures of logic,
but with creatures of emotion.
DALE CARNEGIE

Never persist in trying to set people right.
HANNAH WHITALL SMITH

MORE FROM GOD'S WORD

If God is for us, who is against us?
ROMANS 8:31 HCSB

The LORD is a refuge for His people and a stronghold.
JOEL 3:16 NASB

God shall wipe away all the tears from their eyes.
REVELATION 7:17 KJV

The LORD is near to those who have a broken heart.
PSALM 34:18 NKJV

Give your burdens to the LORD, and he will take care of you.
He will not permit the godly to slip and fall.
PSALM 55:22 NLT

A TIMELY TIP

If you're caught in a troubled relationship, don't be discouraged and
don't give up hope. There's always something you can do to make
your life better, even if it means breaking off the relationship. Tough
times never last, but determined, optimistic, faith-filled people do.

22

DISAPPOINTMENTS

WHEN YOU'RE DISAPPOINTED, HE CAN HEAL YOUR HEART

*Then they cried out to the LORD in their trouble,
and He saved them out of their distresses.*

PSALM 107:13 NKJV

From time to time, all of us face life-altering disappointments that leave us breathless. Oftentimes these disappointments come unexpectedly, leaving us with more questions than answers. But even when we don't have all the answers—or, for that matter, even when we don't seem to have any of the answers—God does. Whatever our circumstances, whether we stand atop the highest mountain or wander through the darkest valley, God is ready to protect us, to comfort us, and to heal us. Our task is to let Him.

Life is a tapestry of events: some grand, some not-so-grand, some disappointing, and some tragic. During the happy times, we are tempted to take our blessings for granted (a temptation that we must resist with all our might). But during life's difficult days, we discover precisely what we're made of. And more importantly, we discover what our faith is made of.

When we are disheartened—on those cloudy days when our

strength is sapped and our hope is shaken—there exists a source from which we can draw perspective and courage. That source is God. When we turn everything over to Him, we find that He is sufficient to meet our needs. No problem is too big for Him.

So, the next time you feel discouraged, slow down long enough to have a serious talk with your Creator. Pray for guidance, pray for strength, and pray for the wisdom to trust your heavenly Father. Your troubles are temporary; His love is not.

MORE THOUGHTS ABOUT DEALING WITH DISAPPOINTMENTS

*Let God enlarge you when you are
going through distress. He can do it.*
WARREN WIERSBE

*If your hopes are being disappointed just now,
it means that they are being purified.*
OSWALD CHAMBERS

*In every difficult situation is potential value.
Believe this, then begin looking for it.*
NORMAN VINCENT PEALE

*We all have sorrows and disappointments,
but one must never forget that, if commended to God,
they will issue in good. His own solution
is far better than any we could conceive.*
FANNY CROSBY

Unless we learn to deal with disappointment,
it will rob us of joy and poison our souls.
BILLY GRAHAM

MORE FROM GOD'S WORD

They that sow in tears shall reap in joy.
PSALM 126:5 KJV

He shall not be afraid of evil tidings:
his heart is fixed, trusting in the LORD.
PSALM 112:7 KJV

My son, do not despise the chastening of the LORD,
nor be discouraged when you are rebuked by Him.
HEBREWS 12:5 NKJV

Many adversities come to the one who is righteous,
but the LORD delivers him from them all.
PSALM 34:19 HCSB

He heals the brokenhearted and binds up their wounds.
PSALM 147:3 HCSB

A TIMELY TIP

When you're discouraged, disappointed, or hurt, don't spend too much time asking, "Why me, Lord?" Instead ask, "What now, Lord?" and then get busy. When you do, you'll feel much better.

23

DOUBT

WHEN YOU HAVE DOUBTS

*Immediately the father of the child cried out
and said with tears, "Lord, I believe; help my unbelief!"*
MARK 9:24 NKJV

Doubts come in several shapes and sizes: doubts about God, doubts about the future, and doubts about your own abilities, for starters. And what, precisely, does God's Word say in response to these doubts? The Bible is clear: when we are beset by doubts, of whatever kind, we must draw ourselves nearer to God through worship and through prayer. When we do so, God, the loving Father who has never left our sides, draws ever closer to us (James 4:8).

Have you ever felt your faith in God slipping away? If so, you are not alone. Every life—including yours—is a series of successes and failures, celebrations and disappointments, joys and sorrows, hopes and doubts. Even the most faithful Christians are overcome by occasional bouts of fear and doubt, and so, too, will you. But even when you feel far removed from God, God never leaves your side, not for an instant. He is always with you, always willing to calm the storms of life. When you sincerely seek His presence—and when you genuinely seek to establish a deeper, more meaningful relationship with His Son—God is prepared to touch your heart, to calm your fears, to answer your doubts, and to restore our soul.

MORE THOUGHTS ABOUT DEALING WITH DOUBTS

We are most vulnerable to the piercing winds of doubt when we distance ourselves from the mission and fellowship to which Christ has called us.
JONI EARECKSON TADA

Have you been tormented with fears and doubts? Bombarded with temptation to sin? Try praising the Lord, and watch Satan flee.
NANCY LEIGH DEMOSS

Ignoring Him by neglecting prayer and Bible reading will cause you to doubt.
ANNE GRAHAM LOTZ

Two types of voices command your attention today. Negative ones fill your mind with doubt, bitterness, and fear. Positive ones purvey hope and strength. Which one will you choose to heed?
MAX LUCADO

We never get anywhere—nor do our conditions and circumstances change—when we look at the dark side of life.
LETTIE COWMAN

More from God's Word

*Such doubters are thinking two different things
at the same time, and they cannot decide
about anything they do. They should not think
they will receive anything from the Lord.*
JAMES 1:8 NCV

In quietness and trust is your strength.
ISAIAH 30:15 NASB

*Those who trust in the LORD are like Mount Zion.
It cannot be shaken; it remains forever.*
PSALM 125:1 HCSB

*But he must ask in faith without any doubting,
for the one who doubts is like the surf of the sea,
driven and tossed by the wind.*
JAMES 1:6 NASB

*Jesus said, "Don't let your hearts be troubled.
Trust in God, and trust in me."*
JOHN 14:1 NCV

A Timely Tip

Are doubts creeping in? If so, increase the amount of time you spend in Bible study, prayer, and worship. The more time you spend with God, the better you'll feel about your future and your faith.

24

EMOTIONAL SWINGS

LEARNING TO DEAL WITH
EMOTIONAL UPS AND DOWNS

*Should we accept only good things from
the hand of God and never anything bad?*
JOB 2:10 NLT

From time to time, all of us experience emotional swings. Even the most even-tempered among us experience natural human emotions such as anger, sadness, anxiety, and fear. Since we cannot eliminate these emotional highs and lows, we should seek to understand them. And we must learn to control our negative emotions before they take control of us.

When you encounter unfortunate circumstances that you cannot change, here's a proven way to retain your sanity: accept those circumstances (no matter how unpleasant), and trust God. The American theologian Reinhold Niebuhr composed a profoundly simple verse that came to be known as the Serenity Prayer: "God, grant me the serenity to accept the things I cannot change, the courage to change the things I can, and the wisdom to know the difference." Niebuhr's words are far easier to recite than they are to live by. Why? Because most of us want life to unfold in accordance with to our own wishes and timetables. But sometimes God has other plans. And if we learn to wait patiently for His plans to unfold—and if we learn to accept the things we simply cannot change—we'll deal more effectively with the ups and downs of life.

When we trust God completely and without reservation, we soon discover that our emotional swings are less dramatic and less painful. Then we can be comforted in the knowledge that our Creator is both loving and wise, and that He understands His plans perfectly, even when we do not.

More Thoughts about Emotions

Treat pain and rage as visitors.
Ben Hecht

Bad temper is its own scourge. Few things are bitterer than to feel bitter. A man's venom poisons himself more than his victim.
Charles Buxton

The truth is that even in the midst of trouble, happy moments swim by us every day, like shining fish waiting to be caught.
Barbara Johnson

Find joy in the ordinary.
Max Lucado

Faith is the art of holding on to things your reason has once accepted in spite of your changing moods.
C. S. Lewis

MORE FROM GOD'S WORD

*For this very reason, make every effort to supplement your faith
with goodness, goodness with knowledge, knowledge with self-
control, self-control with endurance, endurance with godliness.*
2 PETER 1:5-6 HCSB

*Grow a wise heart—you'll do yourself a favor;
keep a clear head—you'll find a good life.*
PROVERBS 19:8 MSG

*And let the peace of God rule in your hearts,
to which also you were called in one body; and be thankful.*
COLOSSIANS 3:15 NKJV

*All bitterness, anger and wrath,
shouting and slander must be removed from you,
along with all malice. And be kind
and compassionate to one another, forgiving one another,
just as God also forgave you in Christ.*
EPHESIANS 4:31-32 HCSB

A TIMELY TIP

If you're experiencing hurtful feelings that just won't go away, it's
time to schedule an appointment with your pastor or with a pastoral
counselor or with a mental health professional. These people can
help you look inside to discover, and then banish, the hurtful
feelings or exaggerated thought patterns that may be triggering
negative emotions and holding you back.

25

EMOTIONS ARE CONTAGIOUS

BEWARE: EMOTIONS ARE CONTAGIOUS

Bad temper is contagious—don't get infected.
PROVERBS 22:25 MSG

Emotional highs and lows are contagious. When we're surrounded by people with positive attitudes, we tend to think positively. But when we're surrounded by people whose emotions are negative, we get infected. Negative feelings can rob us of the peace and abundance that would otherwise be ours through Christ. When anger or anxiety separates us from the spiritual blessings that God has in store, we must rethink our priorities. And we must place faith above feelings.

Human emotions are highly variable, decidedly unpredictable, and often unreliable. Our emotions are like the weather, only sometimes far more fickle. As a consequence, we must learn to live by faith, not by the ups and downs of our neighbors' emotional roller coasters. So here's a question you should ask yourself: Who's pulling my emotional strings? Are you allowing highly emotional people or highly charged situations to dictate your moods, or are you wiser than that?

Sometime during the coming day, you may encounter a tough

situation or a difficult person. And as a result, you may be gripped by a strong negative emotion. Distrust it. Rein it in. Test it. And turn it over to God. Your emotions will inevitably change; God will not. So trust Him completely. When you do, you'll be surprised at how quickly those negative feelings can evaporate into thin air.

More Thoughts about Emotions

Our feelings do not affect God's facts.
Amy Carmichael

A life lived in God is not lived on the plane of feelings, but of the will.
Elisabeth Elliot

If you desire to improve your physical well-being and your emotional outlook, increasing your faith can help you.
John Maxwell

Our emotions can lie to us, and we need to counter our emotions with truth.
Billy Graham

It is Christ who is to be exalted, not our feelings. We will know Him by obedience, not by emotions. Our love will be shown by obedience, not by how good we feel about God at a given moment.
Elisabeth Elliot

More from God's Word

But stay away from those who have foolish
arguments and talk about useless family histories
and argue and quarrel about the law.
Those things are worth nothing and will not help anyone.
TITUS 3:9 NCV

Fools give full vent to their rage,
but the wise bring calm in the end.
PROVERBS 29:11 NIV

Stop being angry! Turn from your rage!
Do not lose your temper—it only leads to harm.
PSALM 37:8 NLT

Mockers inflame a city, but the wise turn away anger.
PROVERBS 29:8 HCSB

Make no friendship with an angry man.
PROVERBS 22:24 NKJV

A Timely Tip

The friends you choose can make a profound impact on every aspect of your life. So choose carefully and prayerfully. And remember that you have every right to select friends who contribute to your spiritual and emotional health.

26

ENThUSIASM

BE ENThUSIASTIC!

Whatever you do, do it enthusiastically,
as something done for the Lord and not for men.
COLOSSIANS 3:23 HCSB

Can you truthfully say that you are an enthusiastic person? Are you passionate about your faith, your life, your family, and your future? I hope so. But if your zest for life has waned, it is now time to redirect your efforts and recharge your spiritual batteries. And that means refocusing your priorities by putting God first.

Each day is a glorious opportunity to serve God and to do His will. Are you enthused about life, or do you struggle through each day giving scarcely a thought to God's blessings? Are you constantly praising God for His gifts, and are you sharing His Good News with the world? And are you excited about the possibilities for service that God has placed before you, whether at home, at work, or at church? You should be.

Norman Vincent Peale advised, "Get absolutely enthralled with something. Throw yourself into it with abandon. Get out of yourself. Be somebody. Do something." His words apply to you. So don't settle for a lukewarm existence. Instead, make the character-building choice to become genuinely involved in life. The world needs your enthusiasm...and so do you.

MORE THOUGHTS ABOUT ENTHUSIASM

Two types of voices command your attention today.
Negative ones fill your mind with doubt, bitterness,
and fear. Positive ones purvey hope and strength.
Which one will you choose to heed?
MAX LUCADO

Those who have achieved excellence
in the practice of an art or profession
have commonly been motivated by
great enthusiasm in their pursuit of it.
JOHN KNOX

Wherever you are, be all there.
Live to the hilt every situation
you believe to be the will of God.
JIM ELLIOT

Developing a positive attitude means
working continually to find
what is uplifting and encouraging.
BARBARA JOHNSON

Be enthusiastic. Every occasion is an opportunity to do good.
RUSSELL CONWELL

MORE FROM GOD'S WORD

Let those who seek the Lord be happy.
Depend on the Lord and his strength;
always go to him for help.
1 CHRONICLES 16:10–11 NIV

Happiness makes a person smile,
but sadness can break a person's spirit.
PROVERBS 15:13 NIV

Rejoice always! Pray constantly.
Give thanks in everything,
for this is God's will for you in Christ Jesus.
1 THESSALONIANS 5:16–18 HCSB

But as for me, I will hope continually,
and will praise You yet more and more.
PSALM 71:14 NASB

Do your work with enthusiasm. Work as if you were serving
the Lord, not as if you were serving only men and women.
EPHESIANS 6:7 NCV

A TIMELY TIP

Look upon your life as an exciting adventure because that's precisely what it can be *and* should be. Today and every day, your challenge is to maintain your enthusiasm for life, even when times are tough. So ask God to help you focus on His blessings, and don't let anybody steal your joy.

27

ENVY

ENVY IS EMOTIONAL POISON

Let us not be desirous of vain glory,
provoking one another, envying one another.
GALATIANS 5:26 KJV

Because we are frail, imperfect human beings, we are sometimes envious of others. But God's Word warns us that envy is sin. Thus, we must guard ourselves against the natural tendency to feel resentment and jealousy when other people experience good fortune.

As believers, we have absolutely no reason to be envious of any people on earth. After all, as Christians we are already recipients of the greatest gift in all creation: God's grace. We have been promised the gift of eternal life through God's only begotten Son, and we must count that gift as our most precious possession.

Rather than succumbing to the sin of envy, we should focus on the marvelous things that God has done for us—starting with Christ's sacrifice. And we must refrain from preoccupying ourselves with the blessings that God has chosen to give others.

So here's a surefire formula for a happier, healthier life: count your own blessings and let your neighbors count theirs. It's the godly way to live.

More Thoughts about Envy

How can you feel the miseries
of envy when you possess
in Christ the best of all portions?
C. H. Spurgeon

Envy and greed always—
always—exact a terrible price.
Billy Graham

The jealous are troublesome to others,
but a torment to themselves.
William Penn

Envy shoots at others and wounds herself.
Thomas Fuller

Resentment always hurts you
more than the person you resent.
Rick Warren

Envy takes the joy, happiness,
and contentment out of living.
Billy Graham

More from God's Word

Don't envy evil men or desire to be with them.
PROVERBS 24:1 HCSB

Do not covet your neighbor's house.
Do not covet your neighbor's wife,
male or female servant, ox or donkey,
or anything else that belongs to your neighbor.
EXODUS 20:17 NLT

Where jealousy and selfishness are,
there will be confusion and every kind of evil.
JAMES 3:16 NCV

Let us not become boastful,
challenging one another, envying one another.
GALATIANS 5:26 NASB

So rid yourselves of all malice,
all deceit, hypocrisy, envy, and all slander.
1 PETER 2:1 HCSB

A Timely Tip

You can be envious, or you can be happy, but you can't be both. Envy and happiness can't live at the same time in the same brain, so guard your thoughts accordingly.

28

ESTABLISHING BOUNDARIES

ESTABLISHING
COMMON-SENSE BOUNDARIES

Stay away from a fool,
for you will not find knowledge on their lips.
PROVERBS 14:7 NIV

When you become involved in relationships that require you to compromise your values, you'll make yourself miserable. Why? Because when you find yourself in situations where other people are encouraging you to do things you know to be wrong, your guilty conscience simply won't allow you to be happy. And if you find yourself surrounded by people who are unstable, impulsive, or addicted, you'll soon discover that emotional distress is contagious, as are its consequences.

In a perfect world populated by perfect people, our relationships would be trouble-free. But the world isn't perfect, and neither are the people who inhabit it. As a consequence, we occasionally find ourselves struggling in less-than-perfect relationships. As we work to make those imperfect relationships a little happier and healthier, we must first try to establish sensible boundaries. And if we find ourselves in relationships that are debilitating or dangerous, we should accept the fact that complete separation may be necessary.

To fully experience God's gifts, you need to establish sensible boundaries with people whose emotional challenges present threats to your emotional or physical health. After all, you deserve relationships that will bring abundance to you, to your family, and to God's world.

MORE THOUGHTS ABOUT ESTABLISHING BOUNDARIES

You are justified in avoiding people who send you
from their presence with less hope and strength
to cope with life's problems than when you met them.
ELLA WHEELER WILCOX

Stay away from fatty foods, hard liquor,
and negative people.
MARIE T. FREEMAN

Not everybody is healthy enough
to have a front-row seat in your life.
SUSAN L. TAYLOR

It is far better to be alone than to be in bad company.
GEORGE WASHINGTON

No one can drive us crazy unless we give them the keys.
DOUG HORTON

MORE FROM GOD'S WORD

Be sober, be vigilant; because your adversary
the devil walks about like a roaring lion,
seeking whom he may devour.
1 PETER 5:8 NKJV

It is better to meet a bear robbed
of her cubs than to meet a fool doing foolish things.
PROVERBS 17:12 NCV

Do not be deceived: "Bad company corrupts good morals."
1 CORINTHIANS 15:33 HCSB

You are not the same as those who do not believe.
So do not join yourselves to them. Good and bad do not belong
together. Light and darkness cannot share together.
2 CORINTHIANS 6:14 NCV

Walk with the wise and become wise;
associate with fools and get in trouble.
PROVERBS 13:20 NLT

A TIMELY TIP

You can't change other people, but you can change the way that you react to them. If someone is threatening you, either physically or emotionally, you have the right to set boundaries and enforce those boundaries, even if it means separating yourself from that person.

29

FAITH

FAITH MAKES THE DIFFERENCE

*And he said unto her, Daughter, thy faith hath
made thee whole; go in peace, and be whole.*

MARK 5:34 KJV

Every life—including yours—is a series of successes and failures,
celebrations and disappointments, joys and sorrows. Every step of
the way, through every triumph and tragedy, God will stand by your
side and strengthen you *if* you have faith in Him. Jesus taught His
disciples that if they had faith, they could move mountains. You
can too.

When a suffering woman sought healing by merely touching
the hem of His cloak, Jesus replied, "Daughter, be of good comfort;
thy faith hath made thee whole" (Matthew 9:22 KJV). The message
to believers of every generation is clear: we must live by faith today
and every day.

When you place your faith, your trust, indeed your life in the
hands of Christ Jesus, you'll be amazed at the marvelous things He
can do with you and through you. So strengthen your faith through
praise, through worship, through Bible study, and through prayer.
And trust God's plans. With Him, all things are possible, and He
stands ready to open a world of possibilities to you *if* you have faith.

MORE THOUGHTS ABOUT MOUNTAIN-MOVING FAITH

*I have learned that faith means
trusting in advance what will
only make sense in reverse.*
PHILLIP YANCEY

*Faith is not merely holding on to God.
It is God holding on to you.*
CORRIE TEN BOOM

*Shout the shout of faith.
Nothing can withstand the
triumphant faith that links itself
to omnipotence. The secret of all
successful living lies in this shout of faith.*
HANNAH WHITALL SMITH

*Faith does not concern itself
with the entire journey. One step is enough.*
LETTIE COWMAN

*Faith points us beyond our problems
to the hope we have in Christ.*
BILLY GRAHAM

More from God's Word

All things are possible for the one who believes.
MARK 9:23 NCV

Don't be afraid, because I am your God.
I will make you strong and will help you;
I will support you with my right hand that saves you.
ISAIAH 41:10 NCV

Blessed are they that have not seen,
and yet have believed.
JOHN 20:29 KJV

Don't be afraid. Only believe.
MARK 5:36 HCSB

For truly I say to you, if you have faith
the size of a mustard seed, you will say to this mountain,
"Move from here to there" and it shall move;
and nothing will be impossible to you.
MATTHEW 17:20 NASB

A Timely Tip

Think you're in an impossible situation? Think again. You still have options, and God can still move mountains. Your job is to let Him.

30

FEAR

FEAR NOT. GOD IS BIGGER THAN YOUR DIFFICULTIES

Fear not, for I am with you; be not dismayed,
for I am your God. I will strengthen you, yes, I will help you,
I will uphold you with My righteous right hand.
ISAIAH 41:10 NKJV

All of us may find our courage tested by the inevitable disappointments and tragedies of life. After all, ours is a world filled with uncertainty, hardship, sickness, and danger. Old Man Trouble, it seems, is never too far from the front door.

When we focus on our fears and our doubts, we may find many reasons to lie awake at night and fret about the uncertainties of the coming day. A better strategy, of course, is to focus not on our fears but instead on our God.

God is as near as your next breath, and He is in control. He offers salvation to all His children, including you. God is your shield and your strength; you are His forever. So don't focus your thoughts upon the fears of the day. Instead, trust God's plan and His eternal love for you. And remember: God is good, and He has the last word.

More Thoughts about Facing Your Fears

God shields us from most of the things we fear,
but when He chooses not to shield us,
He unfailingly allots grace in the measure needed.
ELISABETH ELLIOT

A perfect faith would lift us absolutely above fear.
GEORGE MACDONALD

The presence of fear does not mean
you have no faith. Fear visits everyone.
But make your fear a visitor and not a resident.
MAX LUCADO

It is good to remind ourselves
that the will of God comes from
the heart of God and that we need not be afraid.
WARREN WIERSBE

God's power is great enough for our
deepest desperation. You can go on.
You can pick up the pieces and start anew.
You can face your fears.
You can find peace in the rubble.
There is healing for your soul.
SUZANNE DALE EZELL

MORE FROM GOD'S WORD

Be not afraid, only believe.
MARK 5:36 KJV

But He said to them, "It is I; do not be afraid."
JOHN 6:20 NKJV

Even though I walk through the darkest valley,
I will fear no evil, for you are with me;
your rod and your staff, they comfort me.
PSALM 23:4 NIV

The LORD is my light and my salvation—
whom should I fear? The LORD is the stronghold of my life—
of whom should I be afraid?
PSALM 27:1 HCSB

Peace I leave with you; My peace I give to you;
not as the world gives do I give to you.
Do not let your heart be troubled, nor let it be fearful.
JOHN 14:27 NASB

A TIMELY TIP

Are you feeling anxious or fearful? If so, trust God to handle those problems that are simply too big for you to solve. Entrust the future—your future—to God. The two of you, working together, can accomplish great things for His kingdom.

31

FOLLOWING CHRIST

FOLLOW IN HIS FOOTSTEPS
AS CLOSELY AS YOU CAN

Then He said to them all, "If anyone wants to come with Me,
he must deny himself, take up his cross daily, and follow Me."
LUKE 9:23 HCSB

Whom will you walk with today? Are you going to walk with people who worship the ways of the world? Or are you going to walk with the Son of God? Jesus walks with you. Are you walking with Him? I hope you will choose to walk with Him today and every day of your life.

Jesus loved you so much that He endured unspeakable humiliation and suffering for you. How will you respond to Christ's sacrifice? Will you take up your cross and follow Him (Luke 9:23) or will you choose another path? When you place your hopes squarely at the foot of the cross, when you place Jesus squarely at the center of your life, you will be blessed.

The nineteenth-century writer Hannah Whitall Smith observed, "The crucial question for each of us is this: What do you think of Jesus, and do you yet have a personal acquaintance with Him?" Indeed, the answer to that question determines the quality, the course, and the direction of our lives today and for all eternity.

Today provides another glorious opportunity to place yourself in the service of the One from Galilee. May you seek His will, may you trust His word, and may you walk in His footsteps—now and forever—amen.

MORE THOUGHTS ABOUT FOLLOWING CHRIST

A disciple is a follower of Christ. That means you take on His priorities as your own. His agenda becomes your agenda. His mission becomes your mission.
CHARLES STANLEY

The crucial question for each of us is this: What do you think of Jesus, and do you yet have a personal acquaintance with Him?
HANNAH WHITALL SMITH

Be assured, if you walk with Him and look to Him, and expect help from Him, He will never fail you.
GEORGE MUELLER

Choose Jesus Christ! Deny yourself, take up the cross, and follow Him, for the world must be shown. The world must see, in us, a discernible, visible, startling difference.
ELISABETH ELLIOT

Christ is not valued at all unless He is valued above all.
ST. AUGUSTINE

More from God's Word

*Whoever is not willing to carry the cross and follow me
is not worthy of me. Those who try to hold on
to their lives will give up true life. Those who give up
their lives for me will hold on to true life.*
MATTHEW 10:38–39 NCV

*Walk in a manner worthy of the God who
calls you into His own kingdom and glory.*
1 THESSALONIANS 2:12 NASB

*Take my yoke upon you, and learn of me; for I am meek
and lowly in heart: and ye shall find rest unto your souls.
For my yoke is easy, and my burden is light.*
MATTHEW 11:29–30 KJV

For we walk by faith, not by sight.
2 CORINTHIANS 5:7 HCSB

*But whoever keeps His word, truly in him the love of God
is perfected. This is how we know we are in Him: the one
who says he remains in Him should walk just as He walked.*
1 JOHN 2:5–6 HCSB

A Timely Tip

When you follow in Christ's footsteps—when you honor Him with
your thoughts, your actions, and your prayers—you can be sure that
you're always on the right track.

32

FOLLOWING YOUR CONSCIENCE

LISTEN CAREFULLY TO KEEP YOUR CONSCIENCE CLEAR

So I strive always to keep my conscience clear before God and man.
ACTS 24:16 NIV

Few things in life torment us more than a guilty conscience. And few things in life provide more contentment than the knowledge that we are obeying God's commandments. A clear conscience is one of the rewards we earn when we obey God's Word and follow His will. When we follow God's will and accept His gift of salvation, our earthly rewards are never ceasing, and our heavenly rewards are everlasting.

Billy Graham correctly observed, "Most of us follow our conscience as we follow a wheelbarrow. We push it in front of us in the direction we want to go." If that describes you, then here's a word of warning: both you and your wheelbarrow may be heading for trouble, and fast.

You can sometimes keep secrets from other people, but you can never keep secrets from God. God knows what you think and what you do. And if you want to please Him, you must start with good intentions, a pure heart, and a clear conscience.

If you sincerely wish to walk with God, follow His commandments. When you do, your character will take care of itself…and so will your conscience. Then, as you journey through life, you won't need to look over your shoulder to see who—besides God—is watching.

MORE THOUGHTS ABOUT FOLLOWING YOUR CONSCIENCE

God speaks through a variety of means.
In the present God primarily speaks by the Holy Spirit,
through the Bible, prayer, circumstances, and the church.
HENRY BLACKABY

Conscience is God's voice to the inner man.
BILLY GRAHAM

The conscience is a built-in warning system that signals
us when something we have done is wrong.
JOHN MACARTHUR

It is neither safe nor prudent
to do anything against conscience.
MARTIN LUTHER

Conscience can only be satisfied if God is satisfied.
C. H. SPURGEON

More from God's Word

Behold, the kingdom of God is within you.
LUKE 17:21 KJV

*Let us come near to God with a sincere heart
and a sure faith, because we have been
made free from a guilty conscience,
and our bodies have been washed with pure water.*
HEBREWS 10:22 NCV

*Create in me a clean heart, O God;
and renew a right spirit within me.*
PSALM 51:10 KJV

*People's thoughts can be like a deep well,
but someone with understanding
can find the wisdom there.*
PROVERBS 20:5 NCV

*Now the goal of our instruction
is love that comes from a pure heart,
a good conscience, and a sincere faith.*
1 TIMOTHY 1:5 HCSB

A Timely Tip

When your conscience speaks, listen carefully. If you consistently live in accordance with your beliefs, God will guide your steps, and you'll be secure.

33

FORGIVENESS

BE QUICK TO FORGIVE

Above all, love each other deeply,
because love covers a multitude of sins.
1 PETER 4:8 NIV

The world holds few if any rewards for those who remain angrily focused upon the past. Still, the act of forgiveness is difficult for all but the most saintly men and women. Are you mired in the emotional quicksand of bitterness or regret? If so, you are not only disobeying God's Word, you are also wasting your time.

Being frail, fallible, imperfect human beings, most of us are quick to anger, quick to blame, slow to forgive, and even slower to forget. Yet as Christians, we are commanded to forgive others, just as we, too, have been forgiven.

If there exists even one person—alive or dead—against whom you hold bitter feelings, it's time to forgive. Or if you are embittered against yourself for some past mistake or shortcoming, it's finally time to forgive yourself and move on. Hatred, bitterness, and regret are not part of God's plan for your life. Forgiveness is.

MORE THOUGHTS
ABOUT FORGIVENESS

*Forgiveness is one of the most beautiful words
in the human vocabulary. How much pain
could be avoided if we all learned
the meaning of this word!*

BILLY GRAHAM

*Forgiveness is an act of the will,
and the will can function regardless
of the temperature of the heart.*

CORRIE TEN BOOM

*Forgiveness does not change the past,
but it does enlarge the future.*

DAVID JEREMIAH

*Look upon the errors of others in sorrow,
not in anger.*

HENRY WADSWORTH LONGFELLOW

*In one bold stroke, forgiveness obliterates
the past and permits us to enter
the land of new beginnings.*

BILLY GRAHAM

Forgiveness is God's command.

MARTIN LUTHER

More from God's Word

The merciful are blessed,
for they will be shown mercy.
MATTHEW 5:7 HCSB

But I say to you, love your enemies,
and pray for those who persecute you.
MATTHEW 5:44 NASB

And whenever you stand praying, if you have anything
against anyone, forgive him, so that your
Father in heaven may also forgive you your wrongdoing.
MARK 11:25 HCSB

And be kind to one another,
tenderhearted, forgiving one another,
even as God in Christ forgave you.
EPHESIANS 4:32 NKJV

Judge not, and you shall not be judged.
Condemn not, and you shall not be condemned.
Forgive, and you will be forgiven.
LUKE 6:37 NKJV

A Timely Tip

Forgiveness is its own reward. Bitterness is its own punishment. Bitter thoughts are bad for your spiritual and emotional health. Guard your words and thoughts accordingly.

34

GOD'S ABUNDANCE

GOD WANTS YOU TO LIVE ABUNDANTLY

I have come that they may have life,
and that they may have it more abundantly.
JOHN 10:10 NKJV

God has a plan for every facet of your life, and His plan includes provision for your spiritual, physical, and emotional health. But He expects you to do your fair share of the work. In a world that is populated by imperfect people, you may find it all too easy to respond impulsively, thus making matters even worse. A far better strategy, of course, is to ask for God's guidance. And you can be sure that whenever you ask for God's help, He will give it.

God's Word promises that He will support you in good times and comfort you in hard times. The Creator of the universe stands ready to give you the strength to meet any challenge and the courage to deal effectively with difficult circumstances. When you ask for God's help, He responds in His own way and at His own appointed hour. But make no mistake: He always responds.

Today, as you encounter the challenges of everyday life, remember that your heavenly Father never leaves you, not even for a moment. He's always available, always ready to listen, always ready to lead. When you make a habit of talking to Him early and often, He'll guide you and comfort you every day of your life.

MORE THOUGHTS ABOUT ABUNDANCE

God loves you and wants you to experience
peace and life—abundant and eternal.
BILLY GRAHAM

Jesus wants Life for us; Life with a capital L.
JOHN ELDREDGE

God is the giver, and we are the receivers.
And His richest gifts are bestowed
not upon those who do the greatest things,
but upon those who accept His abundance and His grace.
HANNAH WHITALL SMITH

Every difficult task that comes across your path—
every one that you would rather not do,
that will take the most effort, cause the most pain,
and be the greatest struggle—brings a blessing with it.
LETTIE COWMAN

Knowing that your future is absolutely assured
can free you to live abundantly today.
SARAH YOUNG

More from God's Word

The Lord bless you and keep you;
the Lord make His face shine upon you, and be gracious to you
NUMBERS 6:24–25 NIV

And God is able to make all grace abound to you,
so that always having all sufficiency in everything,
you may have an abundance for every good deed.
2 CORINTHIANS 9:8 NASB

My cup runs over. Surely goodness and mercy
shall follow me all the days of my life;
and I will dwell in the house of the LORD forever.
PSALM 23:5–6 NKJV

Success, success to you, and success
to those who help you, for your God will help you.
1 CHRONICLES 12:18 NIV

Until now you have asked for nothing in My name.
Ask and you will receive, that your joy may be complete.
JOHN 16:24 HCSB

A Timely Tip

God's blessings are always available. Even when you're dealing with a situation that has unsettled your emotions, the Lord is constantly offering you His abundance and His peace. So remember that you can still find peace amid the storm if you guard your thoughts, do your best, and leave the rest up to Him.

35

GOD'S GUIDANCE

LET GOD BE YOUR GUIDE

*Trust in the LORD with all your heart, and lean not
on your own understanding; in all your ways
acknowledge Him, and He shall direct your paths.*

PROVERBS 3:5–6 NKJV

If you're dealing with negative emotions or troubling circumstances, you need God's guidance. And of this you can be sure: if you seek His guidance, He will give it.

C. S. Lewis observed, "I don't doubt that the Holy Spirit guides your decisions from within when you make them with the intention of pleasing God. The error would be to think that He speaks only within, whereas in reality He speaks also through Scripture, the Church, Christian friends, and books." These words remind us that God has many ways to make Himself known. Our challenge is to make ourselves open to His instruction.

If you're wise, you'll form the habit of speaking to God early and often. But you won't stop there—you'll also study God's Word, you'll obey God's commandments, and you'll associate with people who do likewise.

So if you're unsure of your next step, lean upon God's promises and lift your prayers to Him. Remember that God is always near—always trying to get His message through. Open yourself to Him every day, and trust Him to guide your path. When you do, you'll be protected today, tomorrow, and forever.

MORE THOUGHTS ABOUT GOD'S GUIDANCE

As you walk through the valley of the unknown,
you will find the footprints of Jesus
both in front of you and beside you.
CHARLES STANLEY

Are you serious about wanting God's guidance
to become a personal reality in your life?
The first step is to tell God that you know
you can't manage your own life; that you need His help.
CATHERINE MARSHALL

God never leads us to do anything
that is contrary to the Bible.
BILLY GRAHAM

When we are obedient, God guides our steps and our stops.
CORRIE TEN BOOM

The will of God will never take us
where the grace of God cannot sustain us.
BILLY GRAHAM

More from God's Word

Morning by morning he wakens me
and opens my understanding to his will.
The Sovereign Lord has spoken to me, and I have listened.
Isaiah 50:4–5 NLT

The Lord says, "I will guide you along the best pathway
for your life. I will advise you and watch over you."
Psalm 32:8 NLT

Shew me thy ways, O Lord; teach me thy paths.
Lead me in thy truth, and teach me: for thou art the God
of my salvation; on thee do I wait all the day.
Psalm 25:4–5 KJV

Teach me to do Your will, for You are my God;
Your Spirit is good. Lead me in the land of uprightness.
Psalm 143:10 NKJV

Yet Lord, You are our Father; we are the clay, and You
are our potter; we all are the work of Your hands.
Isaiah 64:8 HCSB

A Timely Tip

When your emotions are frayed or you feel like you're losing control, call time-out and pray for guidance. When you seek it, God will give it.

36

GOD'S PLAN

HE HAS A PLAN FOR YOU

But as it is written: What eye did not see and ear did not hear,
and what never entered the human mind—
God prepared this for those who love Him.

1 CORINTHIANS 2:9 HCSB

Do you want to experience a life filled with abundance, peace, and emotional stability? If so, here's a word of warning: you'll need to resist the temptation to do things "your way" and commit, instead, to do things God's way.

God has plans for your life. Big plans. But He won't force you to follow His will; to the contrary, He has given you free will, the ability to make decisions on your own. With the freedom to choose comes the responsibility of living with the consequences of the choices you make.

When you make the decision to seek God's will for your life, you will contemplate His Word, and you will be watchful for His signs. You will associate with fellow believers who will encourage your spiritual growth. And, you will listen to that inner voice that speaks to you in the quiet moments of your daily devotionals.

Sometimes God's plans are crystal clear, but other times He

leads you through the wilderness before He delivers you to the Promised Land. So be patient, keep searching, and keep praying. If you do, then in time God will answer your prayers and make His plans known. The Lord intends to use you in wonderful, unexpected ways. You'll discover those plans by doing things His way...and you'll be eternally grateful that you did.

More Thoughts about God's Plan

*Every experience God gives us, every person
He brings into our lives, is the perfect preparation
for the future that only He can see.*
Corrie ten Boom

*God's purpose is greater than our problems,
our pain, and even our sin.*
Rick Warren

*If not a sparrow falls upon the ground
without your Father, you have reason
to see the smallest events of your
career are arranged by Him.*
C. H. Spurgeon

*God has a course mapped out for your life,
and all the inadequacies in the world
will not change His mind.
He will be with you every step of the way.*
Charles Stanley

More from God's Word

We must do the works of Him who sent Me while it is day.
Night is coming when no one can work.
JOHN 9:4 HCSB

And yet, O LORD, you are our Father. We are the clay,
and you are the potter. We all are formed by your hand.
ISAIAH 64:8 NLT

It is God who is at work in you,
both to will and to work for His good pleasure.
PHILIPPIANS 2:13 NASB

For whoever does the will of God is
My brother and My sister and mother.
MARK 3:35 NKJV

For My thoughts are not your thoughts, and your ways are not
My ways.... For as heaven is higher than earth, so My ways are
higher than your ways, and My thoughts than your thoughts.
ISAIAH 55:8–9 HCSB

A Timely Tip

Even when times are tough, you can be sure that God has a wonderful plan for your life. And the time to start looking for that plan—and living it—is now. Discovering God's plan begins with prayer, but it doesn't end there. You've also got to work at it.

37

GOD'S PRESENCE

GOD IS ALWAYS WITH YOU

Draw near to God, and He will draw near to you.
JAMES 4:8 HCSB

If God is everywhere, why does He sometimes seem so far away? The answer to that question, of course, has nothing to do with God and everything to do with us.

When we begin each day with prayer and praise, God often seems very near indeed. But if we ignore God's presence or—worse yet—rebel against it altogether, the world in which we live becomes a spiritual and emotional wasteland.

Are you tired, discouraged, or fearful? Be comforted because God is with you. Are you anxious or confused? Listen to the quiet voice of your heavenly Father. Are you bitter? Talk with God and seek His guidance. Are you celebrating a great victory? Thank God and praise Him. He is the Giver of all things good.

In whatever condition you find yourself, wherever you are, whether you are happy or sad, victorious or vanquished, troubled or triumphant, celebrate God's presence. And be comforted. God is not just near. He is here.

More Thoughts about God's Presence

It is God to whom and with whom we travel,
and while He is the end of our journey,
He is also at every stopping place.
ELISABETH ELLIOT

Do not limit the limitless God!
With Him, face the future unafraid
because you are never alone.
LETTIE COWMAN

God is an infinite circle
whose center is everywhere.
ST. AUGUSTINE

Mark it down.
You will never go where God is not.
MAX LUCADO

The Lord is the one who travels
every mile of the wilderness way
as our leader, cheering us, supporting
and supplying and fortifying us.
ELISABETH ELLIOT

More from God's Word

I am not alone, because the Father is with Me.
JOHN 16:32 NKJV

Be still, and know that I am God.
PSALM 46:10 KJV

Though I walk through the valley of the shadow of death,
I will fear no evil: for thou art with me.
PSALM 23:4 KJV

I know the LORD is always with me.
I will not be shaken, for he is right beside me.
PSALM 16:8 NLT

For the eyes of Yawheh roam throughout
the earth to show Himself strong
for those whose hearts are completely His.
2 CHRONICLES 16:9 HCSB

A Timely Tip

The next time you feel a flood of negative emotions coming on, take a deep breath and remind yourself that God isn't far away. He's right here, right now. And He's willing to talk to you right here, right now.

38

GOD'S PROMISES

TRUST GOD'S PROMISES

As for God, his way is perfect: the word of the LORD is tried:
he is a buckler to all those that trust in him.

PSALM 18:30 KJV

In the eighteenth psalm, David teaches us that God is trustworthy. Simply put, when God makes a promise, He keeps it.

So what do you expect from the day ahead? Are you willing to trust God completely or are you living beneath a cloud of doubt and fear? God's Word makes it clear: you should trust Him and His promises, and when you do, you can live courageously.

For thoughtful Christians, every day begins and ends with God's Son and God's promises. When we accept Christ into our hearts, God promises us the opportunity for earthly peace and spiritual abundance. But more importantly, God promises us the priceless gift of eternal life.

Sometimes, especially when we find ourselves caught in the inevitable entanglements of life, we fail to trust God completely.

Are you tired, discouraged, or fearful? Be comforted and trust the promises that God has made to you. Are you worried or anxious? Be confident in God's power. Do you see a difficult future ahead?

Be courageous and call upon God. He will protect you and then use you according to His purposes. Are you confused? Listen to the quiet voice of your heavenly Father. He is not a God of confusion. Talk with Him; listen to Him; trust Him, and trust His promises. He is steadfast, and He is your Protector, now and forever.

MORE THOUGHTS ABOUT GOD'S PROMISES

Let God's promises shine on your problems.
CORRIE TEN BOOM

Beloved, God's promises can never fail to be accomplished,
and those who patiently wait can never be disappointed,
for a believing faith leads to realization.
LETTIE COWMAN

Gather the riches of God's promises.
Nobody can take away from you those texts
from the Bible which you have learned by heart.
CORRIE TEN BOOM

The Bible is God's book of promises, and unlike the books
of man, it does not change or go out of date.
BILLY GRAHAM

Don't let obstacles along the road to eternity
shake your confidence in God's promises.
DAVID JEREMIAH

More from God's Word

He heeded their prayer,
because they put their trust in Him.
1 Chronicles 5:20 NKJV

Sustain me as You promised, and I will live;
do not let me be ashamed of my hope.
Psalm 119:116 HCSB

My God is my rock,
in whom I take refuge,
my shield and the horn of my salvation.
2 Samuel 22:2–3 NIV

They will bind themselves
to the Lord with an eternal covenant
that will never again be forgotten.
Jeremiah 50:5 NLT

Let us hold on to the confession
of our hope without wavering,
for He who promised is faithful.
Hebrews 10:23 HCSB

A Timely Tip

God has made many promises to you, and He will keep every single one of them. Your job is to trust God's Word and to live accordingly.

39

God's Timing

Trust God's Timing

Therefore humble yourselves under the mighty hand of God,
that He may exalt you in due time.
1 PETER 5:6 NKJV

If you're involved in a difficult relationship—or if you're experiencing tough times—you're undoubtedly eager for things to improve. Perhaps you've prayed about your situation but seen no results. If so, keep praying, keep working, and be patient.

The Bible teaches us to trust God's timing in all matters, but we are sorely tempted to do otherwise, especially when our hearts are breaking. We pray (and trust) that we will find peace someday, and we want it now. God, however, works on His own timetable, and His schedule does not always coincide with ours.

God's plans are perfect; ours most certainly are not. Thus we must learn to trust the Father in good times and hard times. So today, as you meet the challenges of everyday life, do your best to turn everything over to God. Whatever your problem, He can solve it. And you can be sure that He will solve it when the time is right.

More Thoughts about God's Timing

Waiting on God brings us to the journey's end quicker than our feet.
LETTIE COWMAN

Teach us, O Lord, the disciplines of patience, for to wait is often harder than to work.
PETER MARSHALL

We must learn to move according to the timetable of the Timeless One, and to be at peace.
ELISABETH ELLIOT

The Christian's journey through life isn't a sprint but a marathon.
BILLY GRAHAM

We often hear about waiting on God, which actually means that He is waiting until we are ready. There is another side, however. When we wait for God, we are waiting until He is ready.
LETTIE COWMAN

More from God's Word

To every thing there is a season,
and a time to every purpose under the heaven.
ECCLESIASTES 3:1 KJV

He has made everything appropriate in its time.
He has also put eternity in their hearts, but man cannot
discover the work God has done from beginning to end.
ECCLESIASTES 3:11 HCSB

Trust in the LORD with all your heart, and lean not
on your own understanding; in all your ways
acknowledge Him, and He shall direct your paths.
PROVERBS 3:5–6 NKJV

Yet the LORD longs to be gracious to you; therefore he will
rise up to show you compassion. For the LORD is a God
of justice. Blessed are all who wait for him!
ISAIAH 30:18 NIV

Those who trust in the LORD are like Mount Zion.
It cannot be shaken; it remains forever.
PSALM 125:1 HCSB

A Timely Tip

If you're waiting patiently for the Lord to help you resolve a difficult situation, remember this: God is never early or late; He's always on time. Although you don't know precisely what you need—or when you need it—He does. So trust His timing.

40

GOD'S WORD

LET HIS WORD BE YOUR LAMP

Your word is a lamp for my feet and a light on my path.
PSALM 119:105 HCSB

As you look to the future and decide upon the direction of your life, what will you use as your roadmap? Will you trust God's Word and use it as an indispensable tool to guide your steps? Or will you choose a different map to plot your course? The map you choose will determine the quality of your journey and its ultimate destination.

The Bible can be the ultimate guidebook for life, and that's precisely how you should use it. So today and every day, make certain that you consult God's instruction book with an open mind and a prayerful heart. When you do, you can be comforted in the knowledge that your steps are guided by a source of wisdom that never fails.

As we face the inevitable challenges of life here on earth, we must arm ourselves with the promises of God's holy Word. When we let His Word be our lamp, we can expect the best, not only for the day ahead but also for all eternity.

MORE THOUGHTS ABOUT GOD'S WORD

The Holy Scriptures are our letters from home.
ST. AUGUSTINE

The Bible grows more beautiful
as we grow in our understanding of it.
JOHANN WOLFGANG VON GOETHE

The Bible is God's book of promises,
and unlike the books of man,
it does not change or go out of date.
BILLY GRAHAM

The Bible is the word of God from cover to cover.
BILLY SUNDAY

The Reference Point for the Christian
is the Bible. All values, judgments,
and attitudes must be gauged in relationship
to this Reference Point.
RUTH BELL GRAHAM

More from God's Word

Jesus answered, "It is written:
'Man shall not live on bread alone,
but on every word that comes from the mouth of God.'"
MATTHEW 4:4 NIV

Therefore everyone who hears
these words of mine and puts them
into practice is like a wise man who
built his house on the rock.
MATHEW 7:24 NIV

For the word of God is living
and effective and sharper
than any double-edged sword,
penetrating as far as the separation of soul
and spirit, joints and marrow. It is able to judge
the ideas and thoughts of the heart.
HEBREWS 4:12 HCSB

A Timely Tip

The Bible contains divine wisdom for dealing with your emotional, spiritual, and physical health. The Lord intends for you to use His Word as a tool to improve your life. Your intentions should be the same.

41

GRATITUDE

AN ATTITUDE OF GRATITUDE

Blessings crown the head of the righteous.
PROVERBS 10:6 NIV

For most of us, life is busy and complicated. We have countless responsibilities, some of which begin before sunrise and many of which end long after sunset. Amid the rush and crush of the daily grind, it is easy to lose sight of God and His blessings. But, when we forget to slow down and say "thank You" to our Maker, we rob ourselves of His presence, His peace, and His joy.

When you're dealing with difficult circumstances, it's easy to focus on your problems, not your blessings. A far better strategy, of course, is to focus on your blessings, not your burdens.

If you tried to count all your blessings, how long would it take? A very, very long time. After all, you've been given the priceless gift of life here on earth and the promise of life eternal in heaven. And, you've been given so much more.

Billy Graham noted: "We should think of the blessings we so easily take for granted: life itself; preservation from danger; every bit of health we enjoy; every hour of liberty; the ability to see, to hear, to speak, to think, and to imagine—all this comes from the hand of God." That's sound advice for believers—followers of the One from Galilee—who have so much to be thankful for. So, it's always the right time to say thanks to the Giver for the gifts you can count *and* all the other ones too.

More Thoughts about God's Blessings

We do not need to beg Him to bless us;
He simply cannot help it.
HANNAH WHITALL SMITH

God is always trying to give good things to us,
but our hands are too full to receive them.
ST. AUGUSTINE

God is the giver, and we are the receivers. And His richest
gifts are bestowed not upon those who do the greatest things,
but upon those who accept His abundance and His grace.
HANNAH WHITALL SMITH

God's gifts put men's best dreams to shame.
ELIZABETH BARRETT BROWNING

God has promised us abundance, peace, and eternal life. These
treasures are ours for the asking. One of the great mysteries of
life is why so many of us wait so long to lay claim to God's gifts.
MARIE T. FREEMAN

More from God's Word

The LORD is my shepherd; I shall not want.
PSALM 23:1 KJV

You will show me the path of life; in Your presence is fullness of joy; at Your right hand are pleasures forevermore.
PSALM 16:11 NKJV

The LORD is my rock, my fortress, and my deliverer, my God, my mountain where I seek refuge. My shield, the horn of my salvation, my stronghold, my refuge, and my Savior.
2 SAMUEL 22:2–3 HCSB

The LORD is good to all: and his tender mercies are over all his works.
PSALM 145:9 KJV

May Yahweh bless you and protect you; may Yahweh make His face shine on you, and be gracious to you.
NUMBERS 6:24–25 HCSB

A Timely Tip

If you're grappling with an uncomfortable situation and your emotions are about to get the better of you, remember this: no matter your circumstances, you are still richly blessed. In fact, God has given you more blessings than you can possibly count, but it doesn't hurt to begin counting them and being grateful. And while you're at it, don't forget to praise the Giver of these incalculable gifts.

42

GRIEF

WHEN YOU GRIEVE,
HE OFFERS COMFORT

*Weeping may endure for a night,
but joy cometh in the morning.*
PSALM 30:5 KJV

Grief visits all of us who live long and love deeply. When we lose a loved one, or when we experience any other profound loss, darkness overwhelms us for a while, and it seems as if our purpose for living has vanished. God has other plans.

The Christian faith, as communicated through the words of the Holy Bible, is a healing faith. It offers comfort in times of trouble, courage for our fears, hope instead of hopelessness. For Christians, the grave is not a final resting place, it is a place of transition. Through the healing words of God's promises, Christians understand that the Lord continues to manifest His plan in good times and bad.

God intends that you have a meaningful, abundant life, but He expects you to do your part in claiming those blessings. So as you work through your grief, you will find it helpful to utilize all the resources that God has placed along your path. God makes help available, but it's up to you to find it and then to accept it.

First and foremost, you should lean upon the love, help, and support of family members, friends, fellow church members, and your pastor. Other resources include

- various local counseling services including, but not limited to, pastoral counselors, psychologists, and community mental health facilities;
- group counseling programs that deal with your specific loss;
- your personal physician;
- the local bookstore or library (which will contain specific reading material about your grief and about your particular loss).

If you are experiencing the intense pain of a recent loss, or if you are still mourning a loss from long ago, perhaps you are now ready to begin the next stage of your journey with God. If so, be mindful of this fact: As a wounded survivor, you will have countless opportunities to serve others. And by serving others, you will bring purpose and meaning to the suffering you've endured.

MORE THOUGHTS ABOUT SADNESS AND GRIEF

God is sufficient for all our needs, for every problem, for every difficulty, for every broken heart, for every human sorrow.
PETER MARSHALL

Despair is always the gateway of faith.
OSWALD CHAMBERS

God has enough grace to solve every dilemma you face, wipe
every tear you cry, and answer every question you ask.
MAX LUCADO

MORE FROM GOD'S WORD

The LORD shall give thee rest from thy sorrow,
and from thy fear.
ISAIAH 14:3 KJV

The LORD is near to those who have a broken heart.
PSALM 34:18 NKJV

Ye shall be sorrowful, but your sorrow shall be turned into joy.
JOHN 16:20 KJV

He heals the brokenhearted and binds up their wounds.
PSALM 147:3 HCSB

Blessed are the poor in spirit: for theirs
is the kingdom of heaven. Blessed are they that mourn:
for they shall be comforted.
MATTHEW 5:3–4 KJV

A TIMELY TIP

Grief is not meant to be avoided or feared; it is meant to be worked through. Grief hurts, but denying your true feelings can hurt even more. With God's help, you can face your pain and move beyond it.

43

GUARDING YOUR HEART

GOD WANTS YOU
TO GUARD YOUR HEART

Guard your heart above all else, for it is the source of life.
PROVERBS 4:23 HCSB

When our emotions get the best of us, we are tempted to respond in vindictive, aggressive ways. Yet God's Word is clear: we are to guard our hearts "above all else." So how should we respond to the difficult people and troubling circumstances that complicate our lives and rouse our emotions? We must react fairly, honestly, maturely, and we must never betray our Christian beliefs.

Here in the twenty-first century, distractions, frustrations, and angry eruptions are woven into the fabric of everyday life. Many famous people seem to take pride in discourteous behavior, and social media has dramatically increased our contact with troubled personalities. As believers, we must remain vigilant. Not only must we resist Satan when he confronts us, but we must also avoid the people and the places where Satan can most easily tempt us.

Do you seek God's peace and His blessings? Then guard your heart. When you're tempted to lash out in anger, hold your tongue. When you're faced with a difficult choice or a powerful temptation, seek God's counsel and trust the counsel He gives. When you're uncertain of your next step, take a deep breath, calm yourself, and follow in the footsteps of God's only begotten Son. Invite God into your heart and live according to His commandments. When you do, you will be blessed today, and tomorrow, and forever.

MORE THOUGHTS ABOUT GUARDING YOUR HEART

There is no neutral ground in the universe:
every square inch, every split second,
is claimed by God and counterclaimed by Satan.
C. S. LEWIS

Our fight is not against any physical enemy; it is against
organizations and powers that are spiritual. We must struggle
against sin all our lives, but we are assured we will win.
CORRIE TEN BOOM

Our battles are first won or lost in the secret places of our will
in God's presence, never in full view of the world.
OSWALD CHAMBERS

No matter how many pleasures Satan offers you, his ultimate
intention is to ruin you. Your destruction is his highest priority.
ERWIN LUTZER

The insight that relates to God comes from purity of heart,
not from clearness of intellect.
OSWALD CHAMBERS

More from God's Word

Finally, brothers and sisters whatever is true, whatever is noble,
whatever is right, whatever is pure, whatever is lovely,
whatever is admirable—if anything is excellent
or praiseworthy—think about such things.

Philippians 4:8 NIV

Flee from youthful passions, and pursue righteousness,
faith, love, and peace, along with those
who call on the Lord from a pure heart.

2 Timothy 2:22 HCSB

The one who keeps God's commands lives in him,
and he in them. And this is how we know that he lives in us:
We know it by the Spirit he gave us.

1 John 3:24 NIV

The peace of God, which surpasses all understanding,
will guard your hearts and minds through Christ Jesus.

Philippians 4:7 NKJV

A Timely Tip

God wants you to guard your heart from situations or harmful emotions that would drive you away from Him. He wants the best for you, and you, of course, want the same for yourself. How do you achieve the best life has to offer? You should start by guarding your heart against the temptations and distractions that threaten your spiritual and emotional health.

44

GUILT

DON'T LET GUILT RULE YOUR LIFE

*Blessed are those who don't feel guilty
for doing something they have decided is right.*
ROMANS 14:22 NLT

All of us have sinned. Sometimes our sins result from our own stubborn rebellion against God's commandments. And sometimes we are swept up in events that are beyond our ability to control. Under either set of circumstances, we may experience intense feelings of guilt. But God has an answer for the guilt that we feel. That answer, of course, is His forgiveness. When we confess our wrongdoings and repent from them, we are forgiven by the One who created us.

Are you troubled by feelings of guilt or regret? If so, you must atone for your mistakes the best you can, and you must ask your heavenly Father for His forgiveness. When you do so, He will forgive you completely and without reservation. Then you must forgive yourself just as the Lord has forgiven you: thoroughly and unconditionally.

More Thoughts about Guilt

*Forgiveness is an opportunity that God
extended to us on the cross. When we accept
His forgiveness and are willing to forgive ourselves,
then we find relief.*
BILLY GRAHAM

*Guilt is an appalling waste of energy;
you can't build on it.
It's only good for wallowing in.*
KATHERINE MANSFIELD

*The purpose of guilt is to bring us to Jesus.
Once we are there, then its purpose is finished.
If we continue to make ourselves guilty—
to blame ourselves—then that is a sin in itself.*
CORRIE TEN BOOM

*The redemption, accomplished for us
by our Lord Jesus Christ on the cross at Calvary,
is redemption from the power of sin
as well as from its guilt. Christ is able
to save all who come unto God by Him.*
HANNAH WHITALL SMITH

*God's mercy is boundless, free, and,
through Jesus Christ our Lord,
available to us in our present situation.*
A. W. TOZER

More from God's Word

See my suffering and rescue me,
because I have not forgotten your teachings.
PSALM 119:153 HCSB

Let us come near to God with a sincere heart
and a sure faith, because we have been made free
from a guilty conscience, and our bodies
have been washed with pure water.
HEBREWS 10:22 NCV

Create in me a pure heart, God,
and make my spirit right again.
PSALM 51:10 NCV

How can I know all the sins lurking in my heart?
Cleanse me from these hidden faults. Keep your servant
from deliberate sins! Don't let them control me.
Then I will be free of guilt and innocent of great sin.
PSALM 19:12–13 NLT

A Timely Tip

Guilt is an emotion that can be debilitating. If you're being plagued by guilt, remember this: If you've asked for God's forgiveness, He has already given it. So if the Creator has forgiven you, why are you unwilling to forgive yourself? When you answer that question honestly, you'll realize that God's forgiveness gives you permission to forgive yourself and move on.

45

HAPPINESS

YES, YOU CAN BE HAPPY

Those who listen to instruction will prosper;
those who trust the LORD will be joyful.
PROVERBS 16:20 NLT

Do you seek happiness, abundance, and contentment? If so, here are some things you should do: love God and His Son; depend upon God for strength; try, to the best of your abilities, to follow God's will; and strive to obey His holy Word. When you do these things, you'll discover that happiness goes hand in hand with righteousness. The happiest people are not those who rebel against God; the happiest people are those who love God and obey His commandments.

What does life have in store for you? A world full of possibilities (of course it's up to you to seize them), and God's promise of abundance (of course it's up to you to accept it). So as you embark upon the next phase of your journey, remember to celebrate the life that God has given you. Your Creator has blessed you beyond measure. Honor Him with your prayers, your words, your deeds, and your joy.

More Thoughts about Happiness

Happiness is a thing that comes and goes.
It can never be an end in itself.
Holiness, not happiness, is the end of man.
Oswald Chambers

Happy is the person who has learned
the secret of being content
with whatever life brings him.
Billy Graham

The practical effect of Christianity is happiness,
therefore let it be spread abroad everywhere!
C. H. Spurgeon

The truth is that even in the midst of trouble,
happy moments swim by us every day,
like shining fish waiting to be caught.
Barbara Johnson

Joy comes not from what we have but what we are.
C. H. Spurgeon

More from God's Word

Joyful is the person who finds wisdom,
the one who gains understanding.
PROVERBS 3:13 NLT

I have come that they may have life,
and that they may have it more abundantly.
JOHN 10:10 NKJV

A joyful heart is good medicine,
but a broken spirit dries up the bones.
PROVERBS 17:22 HCSB

Happiness makes a person smile,
but sadness can break a person's spirit.
PROVERBS 15:13 NCV

If they obey and serve him, they will spend the rest of their days
in prosperity and their years in contentment.
JOB 36:11 NIV

A Timely Tip

The best day to be happy is this one. Even if you're dealing with a difficult situation, you have many reasons to celebrate, so don't delay. Let the celebration begin today. Make up your mind to be happy, and ask God to help you make the choice to rejoice.

46

HATE

HATE IS A SPIRITUAL SICKNESS

*He who says he is in the light, and hates his brother,
is in darkness until now.*

1 JOHN 2:9 NKJV

In Deuteronomy 5:17, God issued a familiar commandment: "Thou shall not kill" (KJV). But Jesus went much further—He instructed us that anger and hatred are akin to murder:

> You have heard that our ancestors were told, "You must not murder. If you commit murder, you are subject to judgment." But I say, if you are even angry with someone, you are subject to judgment!
> (Matthew 5:21–22 NLT).

If you're like most people, you know a thing or two (or three) about anger—and maybe even a thing or two about hatred. Sometimes it's easy to become angry, and it's just as easy to hold a grudge. But God does not want your heart to be hardened by bitterness. He has far better plans for you. So if you bear bitterness against anyone, take your bitterness to God and leave it there. If you are angry, pray for God's healing hand to calm your spirit. If you are troubled by some past injustice, read God's Word and remember His commandment to forgive. When you follow that commandment and sincerely forgive those who have hurt you, you'll discover that a heavy burden has been lifted from your shoulders. And you'll discover that although forgiveness is indeed difficult, with God's help, all things are possible.

MORE THOUGHTS ABOUT HATE

Jesus had a loving heart. If He dwells within us,
hatred and bitterness will never rule us.
BILLY GRAHAM

Give me such love for God and men
as will blot out all hatred and bitterness.
DIETRICH BONHOEFFER

Life is certainly too brief to waste
even a single moment on animosity.
CARDINAL JOSEPH BERNADINE

Love makes everything lovely;
hate concentrates itself on the one thing hated.
GEORGE MACDONALD

I will not permit any man to narrow
and degrade my soul by making me hate him.
BOOKER T. WASHINGTON

More from God's Word

*My dear brothers and sisters, always be willing to listen
and slow to speak. Do not become angry easily, because anger
will not help you live the right kind of life God wants.*
JAMES 1:19–20 NCV

*Everyone must be quick to hear, slow to speak, and slow to
anger, for man's anger does not accomplish God's righteousness.*
JAMES 1:19-20 HCSB

*If anyone claims, "I am living in the light," but hates
a fellow believer, that person is still living in darkness.*
1 JOHN 2:9 NLT

*You have heard it said, "Love your neighbor
and hate your enemy." But I tell you, Love your enemies
and pray for those who persecute you,
that you may be children of your Father in heaven.*
MATTHEW 5:43–45 NIV

A Timely Tip

Life's too short to spend it nurturing hateful thoughts. So if you are
troubled by some past injustice, read God's Word and remember His
commandment to forgive. When you follow that commandment
and sincerely forgive those who have hurt you, you'll discover that
a heavy burden has been lifted from your shoulders. And you'll
discover that although forgiveness is indeed difficult, with God's
help, all things are possible.

47

HOPE

NEVER LOSE HOPE

Let us hold fast the confession of our hope without wavering,
for He who promised is faithful.
HEBREWS 10:23 NASB

On the darkest days of our lives, we may be confronted with an illusion that seems very real indeed: the illusion of hopelessness. Try though we might, we simply can't envision a solution to our problems, and we fall into the darkness of despair. During these times, we may question God—His love, His presence, even His very existence. Despite God's promises, despite Christ's love, and despite our many blessings, we may envision little or no hope for the future. These dark days can be dangerous times for us and for our loved ones.

If you find yourself falling into the spiritual traps of worry and discouragement, seek the encouraging words of fellow Christians and the healing touch of Jesus. After all, it was Christ who promised, "These things I have spoken unto you, that in me ye might have peace. In the world ye shall have tribulation: but be of good cheer; I have overcome the world" (John 16:33 KJV).

Can you place your future into the hands of a loving and

all-knowing God? Can you live amid the uncertainties of today, knowing that God has dominion over all your tomorrows? Can you summon the faith to trust God in good times and hard times? If you can, you are wise and you are blessed.

Once you've made the decision to trust God completely, it's time to get busy. The willingness to take action—even if the outcome of that action is uncertain—is an effective way to combat hopelessness. When you decide to roll up your sleeves and begin solving your own problems, you'll feel empowered, and you may see the first real glimmer of hope.

So today and every day, ask God for these things: clear perspective, mountain-moving faith, and the courage to do what needs doing. After all, no problem is too big for God. Through Him, all things are possible.

More Thoughts about Hope

Of course you will encounter trouble.
But behold a God of power who can take any evil
and turn it into a door of hope.
CATHERINE MARSHALL

The presence of hope in the invincible sovereignty
of God drives out fear.
JOHN PIPER

Jesus gives us hope because He keeps us company,
has a vision, and knows the way we should go.
MAX LUCADO

The earth's troubles fade in the light of heaven's hope.
BILLY GRAHAM

MORE FROM GOD'S WORD

Be strong and courageous,
all you who put your hope in the LORD.
PSALM 31:24 HCSB

I say to myself, "The LORD is mine, so I hope in him."
LAMENTATIONS 3:24 NCV

Hope deferred makes the heart sick.
PROVERBS 13:12 NKJV

The LORD is good to those who wait for Him,
to the soul who seeks Him. It is good that one
should hope and wait quietly for the salvation of the LORD.
LAMENTATIONS 3:25–26 NKJV

This hope we have as an anchor of the soul,
a hope both sure and steadfast.
HEBREWS 6:19 NASB

A TIMELY TIP

If you're worried about dealing with a difficult situation, don't give up hope, and don't stop looking for a better solution to your problems. You and God, working together, can do amazing things. So be hopeful.

48

IMPULSIVITY

TOO IMPULSIVE?

Don't let your spirit rush to be angry,
for anger abides in the heart of fools.
ECCLESIASTES 7:9 HCSB

The Bible teaches us to be cautious, to be careful, and to be prudent. But the world often tempts us to be imprudent and impetuous. The world is brimming with temptations that encourage us to behave recklessly, without preparation or forethought. These are temptations that we must resist.

When you find yourself in a troubling situation, do you sometimes react first then think second? If so, it's worth reminding yourself that rash reactions often have unfortunate consequences.

So the next time you're tempted to make an impulsive decision, slow down, think things over, and contemplate the consequences of your behavior before you act, not after. When you make a habit of thinking first and acting second, you'll be comforted in the knowledge that you're incorporating God's wisdom into the fabric of your life. And you'll earn the rewards that the Creator inevitably bestows upon those who take the time to look—and to think—before they leap.

More Thoughts about Impulsivity

Patience is the companion of wisdom.
St. Augustine

Nothing is more terrible than activity without insight.
Thomas Carlyle

We must learn to wait.
There is grace supplied to the one who waits.
Lettie Cowman

Zeal without knowledge is fire without light.
Thomas Fuller

In times of uncertainty, wait. Always,
if you have any doubt, wait.
Do not force yourself to any action.
If you have a restraint in your spirit,
wait until all is clear,
and do not go against it.
Lettie Cowman

More from God's Word

*A prudent person foresees danger
and takes precautions. the simpleton
goes blindly on and suffers the consequences.*
PROVERBS 22:3 NLT

*Do you see a man who speaks too soon?
There is more hope for a fool than for him.*
PROVERBS 29:20 HCSB

A patient spirit is better than a proud spirit.
ECCLESIASTES 7:8 HCSB

*Those who guard their lips preserve their lives,
but those who speak rashly will come to ruin.*
PROVERBS 13:3 NIV

*Enthusiasm without knowledge is no good;
haste makes mistakes.*
PROVERBS 19:2 NLT

A Timely Tip

When you find yourself in a frustrating situation, you may be tempted to strike back in anger. Resist that temptation. Instead, catch yourself, slow down, and think before you act. When you take time to think about your reactions—and pray about them—you'll make smarter choices.

49

INTEGRITY

DON'T COMPROMISE YOURSELF

The godly are directed by honesty.
PROVERBS 11:5 NLT

Oswald Chambers, the author of the Christian classic devotional text *My Utmost for His Highest*, advised, "Never support an experience which does not have God as its source, and faith in God as its result." These words serve as a powerful reminder that, as Christians, we are called to walk with God and obey His commandments. But we live in a world that presents us with countless temptations to stray far from God's path. We Christians, when confronted with sins of any kind, have clear instructions: walk—or better yet, run— in the opposite direction.

It has been said that character is what we are when nobody is watching. How true. When we do things that we know aren't right, we try to hide them from our families and friends. But even if we successfully conceal our sins from the world, we can never conceal our sins from God.

If you sincerely wish to walk with your Creator, follow His commandments. When you do, your character will take care of itself...and you won't need to look over your shoulder to see who, besides God, is watching.

More Thoughts about Maintaining Your Integrity

Let your words be the genuine picture of your heart.
John Wesley

Character is built over a lifetime.
Elizabeth George

True greatness is not measured
by the headlines or wealth.
The inner character of a person
is the true measure of lasting greatness.
Billy Graham

Character is what you are in the dark.
D. L. Moody

Remember that your character
is the sum total of your habits.
Rick Warren

Have a scrupulous anxiety to do right.
Joseph Pulitzer

More from God's Word

Let integrity and uprightness
preserve me, for I wait for You.
PSALM 25:21 NKJV

The integrity of the upright guides them,
but the perversity of the treacherous destroys them.
PROVERBS 11:3 HCSB

The godly walk with integrity;
blessed are their children who follow them.
PROVERBS 20:7 NLT

He stores up success for the upright;
He is a shield for those who live with integrity.
PROVERBS 2:7 HCSB

Whoever walks in integrity walks securely,
but whoever takes crooked paths will be found out.
PROVERBS 10:9 NIV

A Timely Tip

People who encourage you to betray your conscience are dangerous to your emotional, physical, and spiritual health. Your best strategy is to avoid anybody who wants you to compromise yourself. Life is too short to bear the weight of a guilty conscience.

50

IRRITABILITY

TOO EDGY?

*But the fruit of the Spirit is love, joy, peace,
longsuffering, kindness, goodness, faithfulness,
gentleness, self-control. Against such there is no law.*
GALATIANS 5:22–23 NKJV

None of us are perfect, so all of us can, on occasion, be victimized by negativity and anger. As a result, all of us can become irritable from time to time. These feelings should be temporary, not permanent features of our individual psychological landscapes.

The path to spiritual maturity unfolds day by day. Each day offers the opportunity to worship God, to ignore God, or to rebel against God. When we worship Him with our prayers, our words, our thoughts, and our actions, we are blessed by the richness of our relationship with the Father. But if we ignore God altogether or intentionally rebel against His commandments, we rob ourselves of His blessings and His peace.

If we study God's Word, if we obey His commandments, and if we live in the center of His will, we will not be angry, irritable, or bitter. Instead, we will be growing Christians, and that's exactly what God wants for our lives.

We must seek to grow in our knowledge and love of the Lord in every season of life. Be thankful that God always stands at the door; whenever we are ready to reach out to Him, He will answer. In those quiet moments when we open our hearts to the Father, the One who made us keeps remaking us. He gives us direction, perspective, wisdom, and peace. And the appropriate moment to accept those spiritual gifts is always the present one.

MORE THOUGHTS ABOUT IRRITABILITY

Anger and bitterness—whatever the cause—
only end up hurting us. Turn that anger over to Christ.
BILLY GRAHAM

Hence it is not enough to deal with the temper.
We must go to the source, and change the inmost nature,
and the angry humors will die away of themselves.
HENRY DRUMMOND

Keep cool; anger is not an argument.
DANIEL WEBSTER

In a controversy, the instant we feel anger
we have already ceased striving for the truth
and have begun striving for ourselves.
THOMAS CARLYLE

We must guard against allowing anger to drag us into sin.
JOYCE MEYER

More from God's Word

A gentle answer turns away wrath,
but a harsh word stirs up anger.
PROVERBS 15:1 NIV

A person's insight gives him patience,
and his virtue is to overlook an offense.
PROVERBS 19:11 HCSB

Patient people have great understanding,
but people with quick tempers show their foolishness.
PROVERBS 14:29 NCV

But I tell you that everyone will have to give account
on the day of judgment for every careless word
they have spoken. For by your words you will be acquitted,
and by your words you will be condemned.
MATTHEW 12:36–37 NIV

A Timely Tip

Because all of us are human, we all experience occasional bouts of irritability. But intense, unrelenting irritability can be a warning sign of an underlying psychological or physiological condition that can be treated with therapy or medication or both. So if you or someone you love is chronically irritable, you should strongly consider seeking professional help before the emotional roller coaster runs off the tracks.

51

JOY

BE JOYFUL!

Rejoice in the Lord always. Again I will say, rejoice!
PHILIPPIANS 4:4 NKJV

The joy that the world offers is fleeting and incomplete: here to-day, gone tomorrow, not coming back anytime soon. But God's joy is different. His joy has staying power. In fact, it's a gift that never stops giving to those who welcome His Son into their hearts.

Psalm 100 reminds us to celebrate the lives that God has given us: "Shout for joy to the LORD, all the earth. Worship the LORD with gladness; come before him with joyful songs" (vv. 1–2 NIV). Yet sometimes, amid the inevitable complications and predicaments that are woven into the fabric of everyday life, we forget to rejoice. Instead of celebrating life, we complain about it. This is an understandable mistake, but a mistake nonetheless. As Christians, we are called by our Creator to live joyfully and abundantly. To do otherwise is to squander His spiritual gifts.

This day and every day, Christ offers you His peace and His joy. Accept it and share it with others, just as He has shared His joy with you.

More Thoughts about Joy

*Joy is the direct result of having God's
perspective on our daily lives and the effect
of loving our Lord enough to obey
His commands and trust His promises.*

BILL BRIGHT

*Joy is the settled assurance that God
is in control of all the details of my life,
the quiet confidence that ultimately
everything is going to be all right,
and the determined choice to praise God in all things.*

KAY WARREN

Joy is the great note all throughout the Bible.

OSWALD CHAMBERS

Joy comes not from what we have but what we are.

C. H. SPURGEON

*When we get rid of inner conflicts
and wrong attitudes toward life,
we will almost automatically burst into joy.*

E. STANLEY JONES

More from God's Word

So you also have sorrow now.
But I will see you again.
Your hearts will rejoice,
and no one will rob you of your joy.
JOHN 16:22 HCSB

Until now you have asked for nothing in My name.
Ask and you will receive,
so that your joy may be complete.
JOHN 16:24 HCSB

I have spoken these things to you
so that My joy may be in you
and your joy may be complete.
JOHN 15:11 HCSB

This is the day which the LORD has made;
let us rejoice and be glad in it.
PSALM 118:24 NASB

A Timely Tip

Joy does not depend upon your circumstances; it depends upon your thoughts and upon your relationship with God. Every day, the Lord gives you many reasons to rejoice. The gifts are His, but the rejoicing is up to you.

52

JUDGING OTHERS
LET GOD BE THE JUDGE

Judge not, and you shall not be judged. Condemn not, and you shall not be condemned. Forgive, and you will be forgiven.
LUKE 6:37 NKJV

The need to judge others seems woven into the very fabric of human consciousness. We mortals feel compelled to serve as informal judges and juries, pronouncing our own verdicts on the actions and perceived motivations of others, all the while excusing—or oftentimes hiding—our own shortcomings. But God's Word instructs us to let Him be the judge. He knows that we, with our limited knowledge and personal biases, are simply ill-equipped to assess the actions of others. The act of judging, then, becomes not only an act of futility, but also an affront to our Creator.

When Jesus came upon a woman who had been condemned by the Pharisees, He spoke not only to the people who had gathered there, but also to all generations. Christ warned, "He that is without sin among you, let him first cast a stone at her" (John 8:7 KJV). The message is clear: because we are all sinners, we must refrain from the temptation to judge others.

So the next time you're tempted to cast judgment on another

human being, resist that temptation. God hasn't called you to be a judge; He's called you to be a witness.

More Thoughts about Judging Others

*Oh, how horrible our sins look
when they are committed by someone else.*
CHARLES SWINDOLL

Yes, let God be the Judge. Your job today is to be a witness.
WARREN WIERSBE

*We must learn to regard people less in the light of what
they do or omit to do, and more in light of what they suffer.*
DIETRICH BONHOEFFER

*Don't judge other people more harshly
than you want God to judge you.*
MARIE T. FREEMAN

Judging draws the judgment of others.
CATHERINE MARSHALL

More from God's Word

Let the words of my mouth and the meditation
of my heart be acceptable in Your sight,
O Lord, my strength and my Redeemer.
Psalm 19:14 NKJV

Therefore, any one of you who judges
is without excuse. For when you judge another,
you condemn yourself, since you,
the judge, do the same things.
Romans 2:1 HCSB

Those who guard their lips preserve their lives,
but those who speak rashly will come to ruin.
Proverbs 13:3 NIV

Don't criticize one another, brothers.
He who criticizes a brother or judges his brother
criticizes the law and judges the law.
But if you judge the law, you are not
a doer of the law but a judge.
James 4:11 HCSB

A Timely Tip

It's easy to judge other people, but if you spend all day judging others, you've wasted your day. So if you catch yourself being overly judgmental, slow down long enough to interrupt those critical thoughts before they hijack your emotions and wreck your day.

53

KINDNESS AND COMPASSION

IT PAYS TO BE KIND

And let us not grow weary while doing good,
for in due season we shall reap if we do not lose heart.
GALATIANS 6:9 NKJV

As Christians, we have certain rules that we must live by. One of those rules is the Golden Rule, which instructs us to treat others as we wish to be treated. It's a simple concept to understand but a decidedly more difficult concept to put into practice, especially when people are behaving badly. Nonetheless, we are instructed to be kind and compassionate to all people, not just the ones who are easy to get along with.

In the busyness and confusion of daily life, it is easy to lose focus, and it is easy to become frustrated. We are imperfect human beings struggling to manage our lives as best we can, but we often fall short. When we are distracted or disappointed, we may neglect to share a kind word or a kind deed. This oversight hurts others, but it hurts us most of all.

Today, as you consider all the things that Christ has done in your life, honor Him by being a little kinder than necessary. Honor

Him by slowing down long enough to say an extra word of encouragement to someone who needs it. Honor Him by following His commandments and obeying the Golden Rule. He expects no less, and He deserves no less.

MORE THOUGHTS ABOUT KINDNESS AND COMPASSION

Want to snatch a day from the manacles of boredom?
Do overgenerous deeds, acts beyond reimbursement.
Kindness without compensation.
Do a deed for which you cannot be repaid.
MAX LUCADO

All around you are people whose lives
are filled with trouble and sorrow.
They need your compassion and encouragement.
BILLY GRAHAM

When we bring sunshine into the lives of others,
we're warmed by it ourselves.
When we spill a little happiness, it splashes on us.
BARBARA JOHNSON

Do all the good you can by all the means you can,
in all the places you can at all the times you can,
to all the people you can as long as ever you can.
JOHN WESLEY

More from God's Word

Assuredly, I say to you, inasmuch as you did it to one of the least of these My brethren, you did it to Me.
MATTHEW 25:40 NKJV

A new commandment I give unto you, That ye love one another; as I have loved you, that ye also love one another.
JOHN 13:34 KJV

Be kind to one another, tender-hearted, forgiving each other, just as God in Christ also has forgiven you.
EPHESIANS 4:32 NASB

Who is wise and understanding among you? He should show his works by good conduct with wisdom's gentleness.
JAMES 3:13 HCSB

Therefore, whatever you want men to do to you, do also to them, for this is the Law and the Prophets.
MATTHEW 7:12 NKJV

A Timely Tip

The Golden Rule starts with you, so be kind to everybody, even when you're feeling anxious or worried. Be sure to treat other folks in the same way that you would like to be treated if you were in their shoes.

54

LEARNING

ALWAYS KEEP LEARNING

Wisdom is the principal thing; therefore get wisdom.
And in all your getting, get understanding.
PROVERBS 4:7 NKJV

Whether you're twenty-two or a hundred and two, you've still got lots to learn. Even if you're very wise, God isn't finished with you yet, and He isn't finished teaching you important lessons about life here on earth and life eternal.

God does not intend for you to remain stuck in emotional or intellectual quicksand. Far from it! God wants you to continue growing as a person and as a Christian every day that you live. And make no mistake: both spiritual and intellectual growth are possible during every stage of life—during the happiest days and the hardest ones.

How can you make sure that you'll keep growing (and learning) during good times and hard times? You do so through prayer, through worship, through fellowship, through an openness to God's Holy Spirit, and through a careful study of God's holy Word.

Your Bible contains powerful prescriptions for emotional health. When you study God's Word and live according to His commandments, adversity becomes a practical instructor. While you're enduring difficult days, you learn lessons you simply could not have learned any other way. And when you learn those lessons, you will serve as a shining example to your friends, to your family, and to the world.

MORE THOUGHTS ABOUT LEARNING

True learning can take place at every age of life,
and it doesn't have to be in the curriculum plan.
SUZANNE DALE EZELL

Learning makes a man fit company for himself.
THOMAS FULLER

Every day we live is a priceless gift
of God, loaded with possibilities to learn
something new, to gain fresh insights.
DALE EVANS ROGERS

Life is not a holiday but an education.
And, the one eternal lesson for
all of us is how we can love.
HENRY DRUMMOND

A time of trouble and darkness is meant
to teach you lessons you desperately need.
LETTIE COWMAN

More from God's Word

*Anyone who listens to my teaching
and follows it is wise,
like a person who builds a house on solid rock.*
MATTHEW 7:24 NLT

*Enthusiasm without knowledge is not good.
If you act too quickly, you might make a mistake.*
PROVERBS 19:2 NCV

*Teach me Your way, Yahweh,
and I will live by Your truth.
Give me an undivided mind to fear Your name.*
PSALM 86:11 HCSB

*Joyful is the is the person who finds wisdom,
the one who gains understanding.*
PROVERBS 3:13 NLT

*Commit yourself to instruction;
listen carefully to words of knowledge.*
PROVERBS 23:12 NLT

A Timely Tip

Every day has its lessons. So today, spend a few minutes thinking about the lessons that God is trying to teach you. Focus on one area of your life that needs attention now. And remember, it's always the right time to learn something new.

55

LEARNING TO MANAGE EMOTIONS

LEARNING TO KEEP EMOTIONS IN CHECK

Grow a wise heart—you'll do yourself a favor;
keep a clear head—you'll find a good life.
PROVERBS 19:8 MSG

Time and again, the Bible instructs us to live by faith. Yet despite our best intentions, difficult people and the negative feelings they engender can rob us of the peace and abundance that could be ours—and should be ours—through Christ. When anger, frustration, impatience, or anxiety separate us from the spiritual blessings that God has in store, we must rethink our priorities. And we must place faith above feelings.

Sometimes, amid the inevitable hustle and bustle of daily living, you may lose sight of the real joys of life as you wrestle with the challenges that confront you. Yet joy is available to people (like you) who learn to seek it in proper places and in proper ways. The thoughts you think, the actions you take, the prayers you pray, and the people you serve all have a powerful influence on your emotions.

Who is in charge of your emotions? Is it you, or have you formed the unfortunate habit of letting other people—or troubling situations—determine the quality of your thoughts and the direction of your day? If you're wise, and if you'd like to build a better life for yourself and your loved ones, you'll learn to control your emotions before your emotions control you.

MORE THOUGHTS ABOUT YOUR EMOTIONS

If you desire to improve your physical well-being and your emotional outlook, increasing your faith can help you.
JOHN MAXWELL

Our emotions can lie to us, and we need to counter our emotions with truth.
BILLY GRAHAM

Our feelings do not affect God's facts.
AMY CARMICHAEL

A life lived in God is not lived on the plane of feelings, but of the will.
ELISABETH ELLIOT

It is Christ who is to be exalted, not our feelings. We will know Him by obedience, not by emotions. Our love will be shown by obedience, not by how good we feel about God at a given moment.
ELISABETH ELLIOT

More from God's Word

All bitterness, anger and wrath, shouting and slander
must be removed from you, along with all malice.
And be kind and compassionate to one another, forgiving
one another, just as God also forgave you in Christ.
Ephesians 4:31–32 HCSB

Enthusiasm without knowledge is not good.
If you act too quickly, you might make a mistake.
Proverbs 19:2 NCV

And let the peace of God rule in your hearts,
to which also you were called
in one body; and be thankful.
Colossians 3:15 NKJV

For this very reason, make every effort
to supplement your faith with goodness,
goodness with knowledge, knowledge with self-control,
self-control with endurance, endurance with godliness.
2 Peter 1:5–6 HCSB

A Timely Tip

Are you sometimes overly emotional? If so, here are the facts: God's love is real; His peace is real; His support is real. Don't ever let your emotions obscure these facts. And when you encounter difficult people or troubling circumstances, step back, say a silent prayer, and let God handle the things you can't.

56

LISTENING TO GOD

LISTENING CAREFULLY TO GOD

Come to me with your ears wide open.
Listen, and you will find life.
ISAIAH 55:3 NLT

Sometimes God displays His wishes in ways that are undeniable. But on other occasions, the hand of God is much more subtle than that. Sometimes God speaks to us in quiet tones, and when He does, we are well advised to listen carefully.

Do you take time each day for an extended period of silence? And during those precious moments, do you sincerely open your heart to your Creator? If so, you are wise and you are blessed.

The world can be a noisy place, a place filled to the brim with distractions, interruptions, and frustrations. And if you're not careful, the struggles and stresses of everyday living can rattle your emotions and rob you of the peace that should rightfully be yours because of your personal relationship with Christ. So take time each day to quietly commune with your Savior. When you do, you will most certainly encounter the subtle hand of God, and if you are wise, you will let His hand lead you along the path that He has chosen.

More Thoughts about Listening to God

If you, too, will learn to wait upon God,
to get alone with Him, and remain silent
so that you can hear His voice when
He is ready to speak to you,
what a difference it will make in your life!
KAY ARTHUR

Prayer begins by talking to God,
but it ends in listening to Him.
In the face of Absolute Truth,
silence is the soul's language.
FULTON J. SHEEN

When God speaks to us,
He should have our full attention.
BILLY GRAHAM

Deep within the center of the soul
is a chamber of peace where God lives
and where, if we will enter it
and quiet all the other sounds,
we can hear His gentle whisper.
LETTIE COWMAN

God's voice is still and quiet and easily
buried under an avalanche of clamor.
CHARLES STANLEY

More from God's Word

Be silent before Me.
ISAIAH 41:1 HCSB

*In quietness and in confidence
shall be your strength.*
ISAIAH 30:15 KJV

*The one who is from God listens
to God's words. This is why you don't listen,
because you are not from God.*
JOHN 8:47 HCSB

Rest in the LORD, and wait patiently for Him.
PSALM 37:7 NKJV

Be still, and know that I am God.
PSALM 46:10 KJV

A Timely Tip

In every stage of life, and in every circumstance, God has important things He's trying to teach you. So listen carefully to your conscience; pay attention to the things you learn in the Bible; and try to learn something new every day. When you do, God will guide you and protect you.

57

LONELINESS

WHEN YOU'RE LONELY

I am not alone, because the Father is with me.
JOHN 16:32 KJV

If you're like most people, you've experienced occasional bouts of loneliness. So you understand the genuine pain that accompanies those feelings that "nobody cares." In truth, lots of people care about you, but at times you may hardly notice their presence.

Sometimes intense feelings of loneliness can be the result of clinical depression. In such cases, it's time to seek professional help. Other times, however, your feelings of loneliness may come as a result of your own hesitation: the hesitation to "get out there and make new friends."

The world is teeming with people who are looking for new friends. And yet, ironically enough, too many of us allow our friendships to wither away, not because we intentionally alienate others, but because we simply don't pay enough attention to them.

Ralph Waldo Emerson advised, "The only way to have a friend is to be one." Emerson realized that a lasting relationship, like a beautiful garden, must be tended with care. Here are a few helpful tips on tending the garden of friendship...and reaping a bountiful harvest:

- Remember the first rule of friendship: it's the Golden one, and it starts like this: "Do unto others..." (Matthew 7:12 KJV).
- If you're trying to make new friends, become interested in them...and eventually they'll become interested in you Colossians 3:12).
- Take the time to reconnect with old friends: they'll be glad you did, and so, too, will you (Philippians 1:3).
- Become more involved in your church or in community service: they'll welcome your participation, and you'll welcome the chance to connect with more and more people (1 Peter 5:2).

More Thoughts about Friendship

Friendship is one of the sweetest joys of life.
Many might have failed beneath the bitterness
of their trial had they not found a friend.
C. H. Spurgeon

What is a friend? A single soul dwelling in two bodies.
St. Augustine

I cannot even imagine where I would be today were it not
for that handful of friends who have given me a heart full
of joy. Let's face it: friends make life a lot more fun.
Charles Swindoll

It is not darkness you are going to, for God is Light.
It is not lonely, for Christ is with you.
It is not unknown country, for Christ is there.
Charles Kingsley

More from God's Word

A friend loves at all times,
and a brother is born for a time of adversity.
PROVERBS 17:17 NIV

As iron sharpens iron,
so people can improve each other.
PROVERBS 27:17 NCV

Oil and incense bring joy to the heart,
and the sweetness of a friend
is better than self-counsel.
PROVERBS 27:9 HCSB

It is good and pleasant when
God's people live together in peace!
PSALM 133:1 NCV

Dear friends, if God loved us
in this way, we also must love one another.
1 JOHN 4:11 HCSB

A Timely Tip

If you're feeling lonely, it's a signal that you need to reach out. Remember that God is close by, and so is someone who needs your help. If you find someone to help, you won't be lonely for long.

58

MENTORS

BE OPEN TO ADVICE

Get all the advice and instruction you can,
so you will be wise the rest of your life.
PROVERBS 19:20 NLT

If you're going through tough times or emotional distress, it's helpful to find mentors who have been there and done that—people who have experienced your particular challenge and lived to tell about it.

When we arrive at the inevitable crossroads of life, God sends righteous men and women to guide us, if we let them. If we are willing to listen and to learn, then we, too, will become wise.

Today, as a gift to yourself, select from your friends and family members a mentor whose judgment you trust. Then listen carefully to your mentor and be open to his or her advice. After all, you still have lots to learn. And the sooner you learn the lesson God is trying to teach you, the better.

MORE THOUGHTS
ABOUT MENTORS

God guides through the counsel of good people.
E. STANLEY JONES

*The next best thing to being wise oneself
is to live in a circle of those who are.*
C. S. LEWIS

*A single word, if spoken
in a friendly spirit,
may be sufficient to turn one
from dangerous error.*
FANNY CROSBY

*It takes a wise person
to give good advice,
but an even wiser person to take it.*
MARIE T. FREEMAN

*The effective mentor strives
to help a man or woman
discover what they can be
in Christ and then holds
them accountable to become that person.*
HOWARD HENDRICKS

MORE FROM GOD'S WORD

Get wisdom—how much better
it is than gold! And get understanding—
it is preferable to silver.
PROVERBS 16:16 HCSB

He whose ear listens to the life-giving
reproof will dwell among the wise.
PROVERBS 15:31 NASB

Plans fail when there is no counsel,
but with many advisers they succeed.
PROVERBS 15:22 HCSB

The wise are glad to be instructed.
PROVERBS 10:8 NLT

A TIMELY TIP

If you find yourself on an emotional roller coaster, don't keep everything bottled up inside. Find a person you can really trust, and talk things over. A second opinion (or, for that matter, a third, fourth, or fifth opinion) is usually helpful.

59

MIRACLES

EXPECT A MIRACLE

Is anything too hard for the LORD?
GENESIS 18:14 NKJV

Do you believe in an all-powerful God who can do miraculous things in you and through you? You should. But perhaps, as you have faced the inevitable struggles of life here on earth, you have—without realizing it—placed limitations on God. To do so is a profound mistake. God's power has no such limitations, and He can work mighty miracles in your own life if you let Him.

Do you lack a firm faith in God's power to perform miracles for you and your loved ones? Have you convinced yourself that your situation is hopeless? If so, you are attempting to place limitations on a God who has none. Instead of doubting your heavenly Father, you must place yourself in His hands. Instead of doubting God's power, you must trust it. Expect Him to work miracles, and be watchful. With God, absolutely nothing is impossible, including an amazing assortment of miracles that He stands ready, willing, and perfectly able to perform for you and yours.

More Thoughts about God's Power to Work Miracles

God specializes in things thought impossible.
CATHERINE MARSHALL

*Faith means believing in realities
that go beyond sense and sight.
It is the awareness of unseen
divine realities all around you.*
JONI EARECKSON TADA

*God's faithfulness and grace
make the impossible possible.*
SHEILA WALSH

*It is wonderful what miracles
God works in wills that are
utterly surrendered to Him.*
HANNAH WHITALL SMITH

God is able to do what we can't do.
BILLY GRAHAM

More from God's Word

For with God nothing shall be impossible.
LUKE 1:37 KJV

What no eye has seen, what no ear has heard,
and what no human mind has conceived"—
the things God has prepared for those who love him.
1 CORINTHIANS 2:9 NIV

You are the God of great wonders!
You demonstrate your awesome power among the nations.
PSALM 77:14 NLT

And Jesus looking upon them saith,
With men it is impossible, but not with God:
for with God all things are possible.
MARK 10:27 KJV

God confirmed the message by giving
signs and wonders and various miracles
and gifts of the Holy Spirit whenever he chose.
HEBREWS 2:4 NLT

A Timely Tip

Nothing is impossible for God. And He's in the business of doing miraculous things. So, never be afraid to ask—or to pray—for a miracle.

60

MISTAKES

DON'T BE TOO HARD
ON YOURSELF

He who covers his sins will not prosper, but whoever confesses and forsakes them will have mercy.
PROVERBS 28:13 NKJV

Everybody makes mistakes, and so will you. In fact, Winston Churchill once observed, "Success is going from failure to failure without loss of enthusiasm." What was good for Churchill is also good for you. You should expect to make mistakes—plenty of missteps—but you should not allow those missteps to rob you of the enthusiasm you need to fulfill God's plan for your life.

We are imperfect people living in an imperfect world; occasional blunders are simply part of the price we pay for being here. But even though mistakes are an inevitable part of life's journey, repeated mistakes should not be. When we commit those inevitable missteps, we must correct them, learn from them, and pray for the wisdom not to repeat them. When we do, our mistakes become lessons, and our lives become adventures in growth, not stagnation.

Have you made a mistake or two or three? Of course you have. But here's the big question: have you used your mistakes as stumbling blocks or stepping stones? The answer to that question will determine the quality of your day and the quality of your life.

More Thoughts about Mistakes

*By the mercy of God, we may repent
a wrong choice and alter the consequences
by making a right choice.*
A. W. Tozer

*Every misfortune, every failure, every loss
may be transformed. God has the power
to transform all misfortunes into "God-sends."*
Lettie Cowman

*God is able to take mistakes,
when they are committed to Him,
and make of them something
for our good and for His glory.*
Ruth Bell Graham

*Mistakes offer the possibility for redemption
and a new start in God's kingdom.
No matter what you're guilty of,
God can restore your innocence.*
Barbara Johnson

It is human to err, but it is devilish to remain willfully in error.
St. Augustine

More from God's Word

Therefore, if anyone is in Christ, he is a new creation;
old things have passed away;
behold, all things have become new.
2 Corinthians 5:17 NKJV

Therefore let us approach the throne of grace
with boldness, so that we may receive mercy
and find grace to help us at the proper time.
Hebrews 4:16 HCSB

Be merciful, just as your Father is merciful.
Luke 6:36 NIV

But the mercy of the Lord is from everlasting
to everlasting upon them that fear him,
and his righteousness unto children's children.
Psalm 103:17 KJV

If we confess our sins to him, he is faithful and just
to forgive us our sins and to cleanse us from all wickedness.
1 John 1:9 NLT

A Timely Tip

Everybody makes mistakes, and so will you. When you fall short of
your expectations, don't overreact and don't be too hard on yourself.
Instead, try to learn something, try to make amends, and try to
move on as quickly as possible.

61

NEGATIVITY

SAY NO TO NEGATIVITY

In my distress I prayed to the LORD,
and the LORD answered me and set me free.
PSALM 118:5 NLT

From experience, we know that it is easier to criticize than to correct; it is easier to find faults than solutions; and excessive criticism is usually destructive, not productive. Yet the urge to criticize others remains a powerful temptation for most of us. Our task, as obedient believers, is to break the twin habits of negative thinking and critical speech.

In the book of James, we are issued a clear warning: "Don't criticize one another, brothers" (4:11 HCSB). Undoubtedly, James understood the paralyzing power of chronic negativity, and so must we. Negativity is highly contagious: we give it to others who, in turn, give it back to us. Be thankful this cycle can be broken by positive thoughts, heartfelt prayers, and encouraging words.

As you examine the quality of your own communications, can you honestly say that you're a booster not a critic? If so, keep up the good words. But if you're occasionally overwhelmed by negativity, and if you pass that negativity along to your neighbors, it's time for a mental housecleaning and verbal makeover. As a thoughtful Christian, you can use the transforming power of Christ's love to break the chains of negativity. And you should.

MORE THOUGHTS ABOUT MAINTAINING A POSITIVE ATTITUDE

*God never promises to remove us from
our struggles. He does promise, however,
to change the way we look at them.*
MAX LUCADO

*Avoid arguments, but when a negative attitude is expressed,
counter it with a positive and optimistic opinion.*
NORMAN VINCENT PEALE

*Developing a positive attitude means working
continually to find what is uplifting and encouraging.*
BARBARA JOHNSON

*The things we think are the things that feed our souls.
If we think on pure and lovely things,
we shall grow pure and lovely like them;
and the converse is equally true.*
HANNAH WHITALL SMITH

*We choose what attitudes we have right now.
And it's a continuing choice.*
JOHN MAXWELL

More from God's Word

I say to myself, "The LORD is mine, so I hope in him."
LAMENTATIONS 3:24 NCV

The LORD is good to those who wait for Him,
to the soul who seeks Him. It is good that one
should hope and wait quietly for the salvation of the LORD.
LAMENTATIONS 3:25–26 NKJV

Hope deferred makes the heart sick.
PROVERBS 13:12 NKJV

Be strong and courageous,
all you who put your hope in the LORD.
PSALM 31:24 HCSB

Make me to hear joy and gladness.
PSALM 51:8 KJV

A Timely Tip

If your inner voice is like a broken record that keeps repeating negative thoughts, you must guard your heart by training yourself to think thoughts that are more rational, more positive, more forgiving, and less destructive. Remember that negative thinking breeds more negative thinking, so nip negativity in the bud, starting today and continuing every day of your life.

62

OVERCOMING TOUGH TIMES

TOUGH TIMES NEVER LAST, TOUGH PEOPLE DO

God blesses those who patiently endure testing and temptation.
Afterward they will receive the crown of life
that God has promised to those who love him.
JAMES 1:12 NLT

As life here on earth unfolds, all of us encounter occasional disappointments and setbacks. Those visits from Old Man Trouble are simply a fact of life, and none of us are exempt. When tough times arrive, we may be forced to rearrange our plans and our priorities. But even on our darkest days, we must remember that God's love remains constant. And we must never forget that God intends for us to use our setbacks as stepping stones on the path to a better life.

When tough times arrive, we have a clear choice: we can begin the difficult work of tackling our troubles...or not. When we summon the courage to look Old Man Trouble squarely in the eye, he usually blinks. But if we refuse to address our problems, even the smallest annoyances have a way of growing into king-sized catastrophes.

We must build our lives on the rock that cannot be shaken: we must trust in God. And then, we must get on with the character-building, life-altering work of tackling our problems because if we don't, who will? Or should?

MORE THOUGHTS ABOUT OVERCOMING TOUGH TIMES

God alone can give us songs in the night.
C. H. SPURGEON

Human problems are never greater than divine solutions.
ERWIN LUTZER

Often God has to shut a door in our face so that He can subsequently open the door through which He wants us to go.
CATHERINE MARSHALL

God is in control. He may not take away trials or make detours for us, but He strengthens us through them.
BILLY GRAHAM

Life is literally filled with God-appointed storms. These squalls surge across everyone's horizon. We all need them.
CHARLES SWINDOLL

All our difficulties are only platforms for the manifestations of His grace, power, and love.
HUDSON TAYLOR

More from God's Word

The LORD is my shepherd; I shall not want.
PSALM 23:1 KJV

I called to the LORD in my distress;
I called to my God.
From His temple He heard my voice.
2 SAMUEL 22:7 HCSB

He heals the brokenhearted and binds up their wounds.
PSALM 147:3 HCSB

The LORD is my rock, my fortress, and my deliverer,
my God, my mountain where I seek refuge.
My shield, the horn of my salvation,
my stronghold, my refuge, and my Savior.
2 SAMUEL 22:2–3 HCSB

We are hard-pressed on every side, yet not crushed;
we are perplexed, but not in despair.
2 CORINTHIANS 4:8 NKJV

A Timely Tip

Perhaps, because you're enduring tough times, you're being forced to step outside your comfort zone. If so, consider it an opportunity to grow spiritually and emotionally. Your challenge is to trust yourself, to trust God, and to follow His lead.

63

PANIC

DON'T PANIC!

So we can say with confidence,
"The LORD is my helper, so I will have no fear.
What can mere people do to me?"
HEBREWS 13:6 NLT

If you've ever experienced a full-blown panic attack, you can attest to the fact that it is a terrifying experience. Your heart beats faster; you can't catch your breath; your emotions are screaming; and you feel frightened beyond words, yet your mind tells you there's nothing to be afraid of. To make matters worse, after you've experienced your first attack, you may develop an ongoing fear of having another one.

Panic attacks occur when we experience an exaggerated physical response to a situation that shouldn't be so threatening. Researchers aren't completely clear on what causes panic attacks, but they can confirm that these are physiological events that include dramatic increases in both heart rate and adrenaline levels. Fortunately, these attacks are highly treatable with counseling, medicine, or both.

So if you've found yourself paralyzed by fear without good reason, don't suffer in silence. Instead, speak with your physician and develop a recovery plan. God wants you to experience His joyful abundance, but untreated panic disorders can get in the way. So don't be afraid or embarrassed to ask for help. It's the surest way to say no to panic and yes to peace.

More Thoughts about Panic

The fierce grip of panic need not immobilize you.
God knows no limitation when it comes
to deliverance. Admit your fear. Commit it to Him.
Dump the pressure on Him. He can handle it.
Charles Swindoll

Are you weak? Weary? Confused? Troubled?
Pressured? How is your relationship with God?
Is it held in its place of priority? I believe the greater the
pressure, the greater your need for time alone with Him.
Kay Arthur

Every misfortune, every failure,
every loss may be transformed. God has the power
to transform all misfortunes into "God-sends."
Lettie Cowman

Even in the winter, even in the midst of the storm, the sun
is still there. Somewhere, up above the clouds, it still shines
and warms and pulls at the life buried deep inside the brown
branches and frozen earth. The sun is there! Spring will come.
Gloria Gaither

More from God's Word

*Peace I leave with you; My peace I give to you;
not as the world gives do I give to you.
Do not let your heart be troubled, nor let it be fearful.*
JOHN 14:27 NASB

*Fear not, for I am with you; be not dismayed,
for I am your God. I will strengthen you,
yes, I will help you, I will uphold you
with My righteous right hand.*
ISAIAH 41:10 NKJV

*The LORD is my light and my salvation—
whom should I fear? The LORD is the stronghold
of my life—of whom should I be afraid?*
PSALM 27:1 HCSB

*Even though I walk tthrough the darkest valley,
I will fear no evil, for you are with me;
your rod and your staff, they comfort me.*
PSALM 23:4 NIV

A Timely Tip

If you experience a full-blown panic attack, don't try to handle it on your own. Instead, talk to your physician. Medical professionals and knowledgeable counselors can offer solutions, but they won't offer them to you unless they're asked.

64

PATIENCE

PATIENCE IS POWERFUL

A person's wisdom yields patience;
it is to one's glory to overlook an offense.
PROVERBS 19:11 NIV

Time and again, God's Word teaches us to be patient and kind. We are commanded to love our neighbors, even when our neighbors aren't very neighborly. But being mere mortals, we fall short. We become easily frustrated with the shortcomings of others even though we are remarkably tolerant of our own failings.

We live in an imperfect world inhabited by imperfect friends, imperfect acquaintances, and imperfect strangers. Sometimes we inherit troubles from these imperfect people, and sometimes we create troubles by ourselves. In either case, what's required is patience: patience for other people's shortcomings as well as our own.

Proverbs 16:32 teaches, it is "better to be patient than powerful; it is better to have self-control than to conquer a city" (NLT). But, for most of us, patience is difficult. We'd rather strike back than hold back. However, God has other plans. He instructs us to be patient, kind, and helpful to the people He places along our path. He instructs to love our neighbors, even the ones who are chronically hard to live with. As believers, we must strive to obey Him, even when it's hard.

THE POWER OF PATIENCE

*Today, take a complicated situation
and with time, patience, and a smile,
turn it into something positive—
for you and for others.*
JONI EARECKSON TADA

Patience is the companion of wisdom.
ST. AUGUSTINE

*Patience graciously, compassionately,
and with understanding judges the faults
of others without unjust criticism.*
BILLY GRAHAM

*Frustration is not the will of God.
There is time to do anything and everything
that God wants us to do.*
ELISABETH ELLIOT

*Bear with the faults of others
as you would have them bear with yours.*
PHILLIPS BROOKS

More from God's Word

The Lord is good to those who depend on him,
to those who search for him.
So it is good to wait quietly
for salvation from the LORD.
LAMENTATIONS 3:25-26 NLT

Be joyful in hope,
patient in affliction,
faithful in prayer.
ROMANS 12:12 NIV

But if we hope for what we do not yet have,
we wait for it patiently.
ROMANS 8:25 NIV

Patience of spirit is better than haughtiness of spirit.
ECCLESIASTES 7:8 NASB

Who among you is wise and understanding?
Let him show by his good behavior
his deeds in the gentleness of wisdom.
JAMES 3:13 NASB

A Timely Tip

When dealing with difficult situations or problematic people, patience pays. Impatience costs. Behave accordingly.

65

PEACE

EXPERIENCING GOD'S PEACE

*These things I have spoken to you, that in Me
you may have peace. In the world you will have tribulation;
but be of good cheer, I have overcome the world.*

JOHN 16:33 NKJV

Have you found the lasting peace that can—and should—be yours through Jesus Christ? Or are you still chasing the illusion of "peace and happiness" that the world promises but cannot deliver?

The Scottish preacher George McDonald observed, "It has been well said that no man ever sank under the burden of the day. It is when tomorrow's burden is added to the burden of today that the weight is more than a man can bear. Never load yourselves so, my friends. If you find yourselves so loaded, at least remember this: it is your own doing, not God's. He begs you to leave the future to Him."

Today, as a gift to yourself, to your family, and to your friends, claim the inner peace that is your spiritual birthright: the peace of Jesus Christ. Christ is standing at the door, waiting patiently for you to invite Him to reign over your heart. His eternal peace is offered freely. Claim it today.

More Thoughts About Experiencing God's Peace

When something robs you of your peace of mind,
ask yourself if it is worth the energy you are expending on it.
If not, then put it out of your mind in an act of discipline.
Every time the thought of "it" returns, refuse it.

KAY ARTHUR

In the center of a hurricane there is absolute
quiet and peace. There is no safer place
than in the center of the will of God.

CORRIE TEN BOOM

Deep within the center of the soul is a chamber
of peace where God lives and where,
if we will enter it and quiet all the other sounds,
we can hear His gentle whisper.

LETTIE COWMAN

Peace does not mean to be in a place where there is
no noise, trouble, or hard work. Peace means to be in
the midst of all those things and still be calm in your heart.

CATHERINE MARSHALL

God's power is great enough for our deepest desperation.
You can go on. You can pick up the pieces and start anew.
You can face your fears. You can find peace in the rubble.
There is healing for your soul.

SUZANNE DALE EZELL

More from God's Word

"I will give peace, real peace, to those far and near,
and I will heal them," says the LORD.
ISAIAH 57:19 NCV

He Himself is our peace.
EPHESIANS 2:14 NASB

But the fruit of the Spirit is love, joy, peace, patience,
kindness, goodness, faith, gentleness, self-control.
Against such things there is no law.
GALATIANS 5:22-23 HCSB

The peace of God, which passeth all understanding,
shall keep your hearts and minds through Christ Jesus.
PHILIPPIANS 4:7 KJV

Peace I leave with you, My peace I give to you;
not as the world gives do I give to you.
Let not your heart be troubled, neither let it be afraid.
JOHN 14:27 NKJV

A Timely Tip

Sometimes peace can be a scarce commodity in a noisy, complicated, twenty-first-century world. But God's peace is always available when you turn everything over to Him. The Lord is ready to renew your strength and give you peace of mind *if* you let Him. The rest is up to you.

66

PEER PRESSURE

SAYING NO TO NEGATIVE PEER PRESSURE

*Do not be mismatched with unbelievers. For what partnership
is there between righteousness and lawlessness?
Or what fellowship does light have with darkness?*
2 CORINTHIANS 6:14 HCSB

Peer pressure can be a good thing or a bad thing, depending upon your peers. If your peers encourage you to make integrity a habit—and if they encourage you to follow God's will and to obey His commandments—then you'll experience positive peer pressure, and that's good. But if you are involved with people who encourage you to do foolish things, you're facing a different kind of peer pressure: the negative kind.

Rick Warren observed, "Those who follow the crowd usually get lost in it." We know those words to be true, but oftentimes we fail to live by them. Instead of trusting God for guidance, we imitate our friends and suffer the consequences. Instead of seeking to please our Father in heaven, we strive to please our peers, with decidedly mixed results. Instead of doing the right thing, we do the "easy" thing or the "popular" thing. And when we do, we pay a high price for our shortsightedness.

Would you like a time-tested formula for successful living? Here is a simple formula that is proven and true: don't give in to negative peer pressure. Period. Instead of getting lost in the crowd, you should find guidance from God. Does this sound too simple? Perhaps it is simple, but it is also the only way to reap all the marvelous riches that the Lord has in store for you.

MORE THOUGHTS ABOUT PEER PRESSURE

Fashion is an enduring testimony to the fact that we live quite consciously before the eyes of others.
JOHN ELDREDGE

Those who follow the crowd usually get lost in it. I don't know all the keys to success, but one key to failure is to try to please everyone.
RICK WARREN

Many Christians give in to various temptations through peer pressure. They find themselves surrendering to worldly passions, justifying pleasures the world offers.
BILLY GRAHAM

Character is always lost when a high ideal is sacrificed on the altar of conformity and popularity.
CHARLES SWINDOLL

More from God's Word

My son, if sinners entice you, don't be persuaded.
PROVERBS 1:10 HCSB

Dear friend, do not imitate what is evil,
but what is good. The one who does good is of God;
the one who does evil has not seen God.
3 JOHN 1:11 HCSB

No, God is the One I am trying to please.
Am I trying to please people? If I still wanted
to please people, I would not be a servant of Christ.
GALATIANS 1:10 NCV

But Peter and the apostles replied,
"We must obey God rather than men."
ACTS 5:29 HCSB

Do not be deceived:
"Bad company corrupts good morals."
1 CORINTHIANS 15:33 HCSB

A Timely Tip

Peer pressure can be good or bad. God wants you to seek out the good and flee from the bad. So if you encounter someone who encourages you to behave badly—or to betray your conscience—run, don't walk, in the opposite direction.

67

PERFECTIONISM

BEYOND PERFECTIONISM

Those who wait for perfect weather will never plant seeds; those who look at every cloud will never harvest crops.... Plant early in the morning, and work until evening, because you don't know if this or that will succeed. They might both do well.

ECCLESIASTES 11:4, 6 NCV

As a citizen of the twenty-first century, you know that demands can be high, and expectations even higher. Traditional media outlets, along with their social-media counterparts, deliver an endless stream of messages that tell you how to look, how to behave, how to eat, and how to dress. And that's only the beginning. If you're not careful, you'll find yourself scrambling to keep up with everybody's expectations, which is impossible.

The world's expectations are impossible to meet; God's are not. God doesn't expect you to be perfect, and neither, by the way, should you.

Remember: the expectations that really matter are God's expectations. Everything else takes a back seat. So do your best to please God, and don't worry too much about what other people think. And when it comes to meeting the unrealistic expectations of a world gone haywire, forget about trying to be perfect—it's impossible.

MORE THOUGHTS ABOUT PERFECTIONISM

God is so inconceivably good. He's not looking for perfection.
He already saw it in Christ. He's looking for affection.
BETH MOORE

The happiest people in the world are not those
who have no problems, but the people who have learned
to live with those things that are less than perfect.
JAMES DOBSON

The greatest destroyer of good works
is the desire to do great works.
C. H. SPURGEON

We shall never come to the perfect man
till we come to the perfect world.
MATTHEW HENRY

What makes a Christian a Christian
is not perfection but forgiveness.
MAX LUCADO

How important it is that we give up our expectations
of perfection in any area of our lives.
FRED ROGERS

More from God's Word

Let not your heart be troubled;
you believe in God, believe also in Me.
JOHN 14:1 NKJV

In thee, O LORD, do I put my trust;
let me never be put into confusion.
PSALM 71:1 KJV

The fear of human opinion disables;
trusting in God protects you from that.
PROVERBS 29:25 MSG

For everything created by God is good, and nothing
should be rejected if it is received with gratitude.
1 TIMOTHY 4:4 NASB

Your beliefs about these things should be
kept secret between you and God.
People are happy if they can do what
they think is right without feeling guilty.
ROMANS 14:22 NCV

A Timely Tip

In heaven, we will know perfection. Here on earth, we have a few short years to wrestle with the challenges of imperfection. God is perfect; we human beings are not. May we live—and forgive—accordingly.

68

PERSEVERANCE

THE POWER OF PERSEVERANCE

Let us not become weary in doing good, for at the proper time we will reap a harvest if we do not give up.
GALATIANS 6:9 NIV

As you continue to seek God's purpose for your life, you will undoubtedly experience your fair share of disappointments, detours, and difficult people. When you do, don't become discouraged: God's not finished with you yet.

The old saying is as true today as it was when it was first spoken: "Life is a marathon, not a sprint." That's why wise travelers (like you) select a traveling companion who never tires and never falters. That partner, of course, is your heavenly Father.

The next time you find your courage tested by unfortunate circumstances, remember that God is as near as your next breath, and remember that He offers strength and comfort to His children. He is your shield and your strength; He is your protector and your deliverer. Call upon Him in your hour of need and then be comforted. Whatever your challenge, whatever your trouble, God can help you persevere. And that's precisely what He'll do if you ask Him. Whatever your problem, God can handle it. Your job is to keep persevering until He does.

More Thoughts
about Perseverance

*Perseverance is not a passive submission
to circumstances—it is a strong
and active response to the difficult events of life.*
Elizabeth George

*Patience and diligence,
like faith, remove mountains.*
William Penn

*Perseverance is more than endurance.
It is endurance combined with
absolute assurance and certainty that
what we are looking for is going to happen.*
Oswald Chambers

*Everyone gets discouraged. The question is:
Are you going to give up or get up? It's a choice.*
John Maxwell

*Success or failure can be
pretty well predicted by the degree
to which the heart is fully in it.*
John Eldredge

*Character consists of what you do
on the third and fourth tries.*
James Michener

More from God's Word

So let us run the race that is before us and never give up.
We should remove from our lives anything that would get
in the way and the sin that so easily holds us back.
HEBREWS 12:1 NCV

We are hard-pressed on every side, yet not crushed;
we are perplexed, but not in despair.
2 CORINTHIANS 4:8 NKJV

For you have need of endurance,
so that when you have done the will of God,
you may receive what was promised.
HEBREWS 10:36 NASB

Finishing is better than starting.
Patience is better than pride.
ECCLESIASTES 7:8 NLT

But as for you, be strong; don't be discouraged,
for your work has a reward.
2 CHRONICLES 15:7 HCSB

A Timely Tip

When tough times arrive, you may be tempted to give up or give in.
Resist the temptation. When you are tested, don't quit at the first sign
of trouble. Instead, call upon God. He can give you the strength to
persevere, and that's exactly what you should ask Him to do.

69

PERSPECTIVE

KEEPING THINGS IN PERSPECTIVE

Since you have been raised to new life with Christ,
set your sights on the realities of heaven, where Christ sits
in the place of honor at God's right hand.
COLOSSIANS 3:1 NLT

For most of us, life is busy and complicated. Amid the rush and crush of the daily grind, it is easy to lose perspective. It's easy, but it's wrong. When our emotions seem to have been hijacked and the world seems to be spinning out of control, we can regain perspective by slowing ourselves down and then turning our thoughts and prayers toward God.

Do you carve out quiet moments each day to offer thanksgiving and praise to your Creator? You should. During these moments of stillness, you will often sense the love and wisdom of our Lord. When you call upon the Lord and prayerfully seek His will, He will give you wisdom and perspective. When you make God's priorities your priorities, He will direct your steps and calm your fears.

So today and every day hereafter, pray for a sense of balance and perspective. And remember: no challenges are too big for God—and that includes yours.

MORE THOUGHTS ABOUT MAINTAINING PERSPECTIVE

God's peace and perspective
are available to you through His Word.
ELIZABETH GEORGE

When you are experiencing
the challenges of life,
perspective is everything.
JONI EARECKSON TADA

Perspective is everything
when you are experiencing
the challenges of life.
JONI EARECKSON TADA

Joy is the direct result of having
God's perspective on our daily lives
and the effect of loving our Lord
enough to obey His commands
and trust His promises.
BILL BRIGHT

The world appears very little
to a soul that contemplates the greatness of God.
BROTHER LAWRENCE

More from God's Word

*Trust in the LORD with all your heart
and lean not on your own understanding.*
PROVERBS 3:5 NIV

If you teach the wise, they will get knowledge.
PROVERBS 21:11 NCV

*Teach me, LORD, the meaning of Your statutes,
and I will always keep them.*
PSALM 119:33 HCSB

*The one who acquires good sense loves himself;
one who safeguards understanding finds success.*
PROVERBS 19:8 HCSB

*Joyful is the person who finds wisdom,
the one who gains understanding.*
PROVERBS 3:13 NLT

A Timely Tip

When you focus on the world, you lose perspective. When you focus on God's promises and His love, you gain clearer perspective. To keep things in perspective, focus on God and on His plans for your life.

70

PESSIMISM

SAY NO TO PESSIMISM

The LORD is my light and my salvation; whom shall I fear?
The LORD is the strength of my life; of whom shall I be afraid?
PSALM 27:1 NKJV

Pessimism is emotional poison. And negativity has the power to harm your heart if you let it. So if you've allowed negative thoughts to creep into your mind and heart, here's your assignment: start spending more time thinking about your blessings and less time fretting about your hardships.

God has promised to protect us, and He intends to fulfill His promise. In a world filled with dangers and temptations, God is the ultimate armor. In a world filled with misleading messages, God's Word is the ultimate truth.

This day, like every other, is a gift from above, filled to the brim with possibilities. But persistent pessimistic thoughts can rob you of the energy you need to accomplish the most important tasks on your to-do list. So today, be careful to direct your thoughts toward things positive. And while you're at it, take time to thank the Giver of all things good for gifts that are, in truth, far too numerous to count.

More Thoughts about Pessimism

Two types of voices command your attention today.
Negative ones fill your mind with doubt,
bitterness, and fear. Positive ones purvey hope and strength.
Which one will you choose to heed?
Max Lucado

Developing a positive attitude means
working continually to find what
is uplifting and encouraging.
Barbara Johnson

Never yield to gloomy anticipation.
Place your hope and confidence in God.
He has no record of failure.
Lettie Cowman

Occupy your minds with good thoughts,
or your enemy will fill them with bad ones;
unoccupied they cannot be.
St. Thomas More

After one hour in heaven,
we shall be ashamed that we ever grumbled.
Vance Havner

More from God's Word

Let us hold fast the confession
of our hope without wavering,
for He who promised is faithful.
Hebrews 10:23 NASB

Make me to hear joy and gladness.
Psalm 51:8 KJV

But if we look forward to something
we don't have yet, we must wait
patiently and confidently.
Romans 8:25 NLT

Let us not become weary in doing good,
for at the proper time we will reap
a harvest if we do not give up.
Galatians 6:9 NIV

But as for you, be strong; don't be discouraged,
for your work has a reward.
2 Chronicles 15:7 HCSB

A Timely Tip

Negative self-talk breeds negative results. Positive self-talk breeds positive results. So as you monitor your thoughts, stay positive. And whatever you do, please don't let chronic pessimism shape your future.

71

PLEASING PEOPLE

YOU CAN'T PLEASE EVERYBODY
(NOR SHOULD YOU TRY)

For am I now trying to win the favor of people, or God?
Or am I striving to please people? If I were still trying
to please people, I would not be a slave of Christ.
GALATIANS 1:10 HCSB

As you seek to discover God's purpose for your life, you will inevitably confront the expectations and demands of life here on earth. Perhaps the pressures of caring for your family or the stresses of building your career have placed a heavy emotional weight upon your shoulders. Whatever your circumstances, remember this: Your first responsibility is to trust God and to obey His commandments. Obedience to Him is determined, not by words, but by deeds. Talking about righteousness is easy; living righteously and responsibly is far more difficult, especially in today's temptation-filled world.

When Jesus was tempted by Satan, the Master's response was unambiguous. Jesus chose to worship the Lord and serve Him only. We, as followers of Christ, must follow in His footsteps. When we place God in a position of secondary importance, we do ourselves great harm. But, when we imitate Jesus and place the Lord in His rightful place—at the center of our lives—then we claim spiritual treasures that will endure forever.

Who will you try to please today: God or man? Your primary obligation is not to please imperfect men and women. Your obligation is to strive diligently to meet the expectations of an all-knowing and perfect God. Trust Him always. Love Him always. Praise Him always. And seek to please Him. Always.

MORE THOUGHTS ABOUT PLEASING PEOPLE

Popularity is far more dangerous
for the Christian than persecution.
BILLY GRAHAM

Don't pay much attention to who is for you
and who is against you. This is your major concern:
that God be with you in everything you do.
THOMAS À KEMPIS

If pleasing people is your goal, you will
be enslaved to them. People can be harsh taskmasters
when you give them this power over you.
SARAH YOUNG

The major problem with letting others define you
is that it borders on idolatry. Your concern to please others
dampens your desire to please your Creator.
SARAH YOUNG

MORE FROM GOD'S WORD

Do not be unequally yoked together
with unbelievers. For what fellowship
has righteousness with lawlessness?
And what communion has light with darkness?
2 CORINTHIANS 6:14 NKJV

It is better to take refuge in the LORD
than to trust in man.
PSALM 118:8 HCSB

Keep your eyes focused on what is right,
and look straight ahead to what is good.
PROVERBS 4:25 NCV

My son, if sinners entice you,
don't be persuaded.
PROVERBS 1:10 HCSB

The fear of man is a snare,
but the one who trusts in the LORD is protected.
PROVERBS 29:25 HCSB

A TIMELY TIP

If you are burdened with a people-pleasing personality, outgrow it. Realize that you can't please all of the people all of the time, nor should you attempt to.

72

POSSIBILITIES

YES, YOU CAN LEARN
TO CONTROL YOUR EMOTIONS

I can do all things through Christ which strengtheneth me.
PHILIPPIANS 4:13 KJV

All of us face difficult days, days when the challenges of everyday life threaten to hijack our emotions. Sometimes even the most optimistic Christians can become discouraged, and you are no exception. If you find yourself enduring difficult circumstances, perhaps it's time for an extreme intellectual makeover—perhaps it's time to focus more on your strengths and opportunities, and less on the challenges that confront you.

Every day, including this one, is brimming with possibilities. Every day is filled with opportunities to grow, to serve, to share, and to rise above unfortunate situations. But if you are entangled in a web of negativity, you may overlook the blessings that God has scattered along your path. So don't give in to pessimism, to doubt, or to cynicism. Instead, keep your eyes upon the possibilities, fix your heart upon the Creator, do your best, and let Him handle the rest.

MORE THOUGHTS
ABOUT POSSIBILITIES

Do not limit the limitless God! With Him,
face the future unafraid because you are never alone.
LETTIE COWMAN

We are all faced with a series of great opportunities
brilliantly disguised as impossible situations.
CHARLES SWINDOLL

Eliminate the word "impossible"
from your conversation;
drop it from your thoughts;
erase it from your attitudes.
Substitute for it that bright
and shining word "possible."
NORMAN VINCENT PEALE

God's specialty is raising dead things to life
and making impossible things possible.
You don't have the need that exceeds His power.
BETH MOORE

A possibility is a hint from God.
SØREN KIERKEGAARD

Alleged "impossibilities" are opportunities
for our capacities to be stretched.
CHARLES SWINDOLL

More from God's Word

Is anything too hard for the LORD?
GENESIS 18:14 KJV

Jesus said to him, "If you can believe,
all things are possible to him who believes."
MARK 9:23 NKJV

Therefore we do not lose heart.
Even though our outward man is perishing,
yet the inward man is being renewed day by day.
2 CORINTHIANS 4:16 NKJV

The things which are impossible
with men are possible with God.
LUKE 18:27 KJV

But Jesus looked at them and said to them,
"With men this is impossible,
but with God all things are possible."
MATTHEW 19:26 NKJV

A Timely Tip

Dealing with roller-coaster emotions can be painful, but with God's help, you're up to the challenge. Keep praying and keep trying to do the right thing. And remember: with God, all things are possible.

73

POST-TRAUMATIC STRESS DISORDER

TREATMENT FOR PTSD IS AVAILABLE AND ESSENTIAL

Blessed are those who mourn, for they shall be comforted.
MATTHEW 5:4 NKJV

Post-traumatic stress disorder (PTSD) is an anxiety disorder that occurs after a highly stressful, deeply disturbing event. People who suffer from PTSD may have insomnia, flashbacks, low self-esteem, and a host of other unpleasant symptoms. They may also experience emotional numbing, hypervigilance, and suicidal thoughts. So it's clear that PTSD is a serious psychological and medical condition that should be treated by trained counselors and medical professionals.

Response to trauma is a highly individualized experience: what's traumatic to one person may not be to another. That being said, there are still certain experiences that make PTSD more likely. People who experience war, assault, a serious accident, or a natural disaster are obviously at risk. Generally speaking, women are at greater risk of PTSD than men.

If you or someone you love has experienced a traumatic event, don't hesitate to ask for help. It's better to seek help and recover than to "tough it out" and suffer. God wants you and your loved ones to experience His abundance. Now.

More Thoughts about Stress

When frustrations develop into problems
that stress you out, the best way to cope is to stop,
catch your breath, and do something for yourself,
not out of selfishness, but out of wisdom.
Barbara Johnson

Stress is as necessary to fine-tuning
in life as it is to fine-tuning a guitar string.
Edwin Louis Cole

The creation of a new heart,
the renewing of a right spirit is an omnipotent
work of God. Leave it to the Creator.
Henry Drummond

Life is strenuous. See that your clock does not run down.
Lettie Cowman

Beware of having so much to do
that you really do nothing at all because
you do not wait upon God to do it aright.
C. H. Spurgeon

More from God's Word

Come unto me, all ye that labour and are heavy laden,
and I will give you rest.
MATTHEW 11:28 KJV

And the peace of God, which transcends
all understanding, will guard your hearts
and your minds in Christ Jesus.
PHILIPPIANS 4:7 NIV

I find rest in God; only he gives me hope.
PSALM 62:5 NCV

Peace I leave with you; My peace I give to you;
not as the world gives do I give to you.
Do not let your heart be troubled, nor let it be fearful.
JOHN 14:27 NASB

You, LORD, give true peace to those who
depend on you, because they trust you.
ISAIAH 26:3 NCV

A Timely Tip

If you suspect that you, or someone you care about, may be suffering from PTSD, please seek professional help immediately. PTSD can be treated with medications or psychotherapy or both. Help is available. Ask for it today.

74

PRAYER

PRAY AND BE ANXIOUS FOR NOTHING

*Be anxious for nothing, but in everything
by prayer and supplication, with thanksgiving,
let your requests be made known to God.*
PHILIPPIANS 4:6 NKJV

Genuine, heartfelt prayer produces powerful changes in us and in our world. When we lift our hearts to God, we open ourselves to a never-ending source of divine wisdom and infinite love.

Is prayer an integral part of your life, or is it a hit-or-miss habit? Do you "pray without ceasing," or is your prayer life an afterthought? Do you regularly honor God in the solitude of the early morning darkness, or do you bow your head only when others are watching?

The quality of your spiritual life will be in direct proportion to the quality of your prayer life. Prayer has the power to change your emotions and to change your life. So make a regular early-morning appointment with the Creator, and keep it. Then, as the day unfolds, continue your conversation with God. Ask Him to give you peace and perspective. When you ask, He will answer. But He's not likely to answer your prayers until you've prayed them.

More Thoughts About Prayer

Prayer begins by talking to God,
but it ends in listening to Him.
In the face of Absolute Truth,
silence is the soul's language.

Fulton J. Sheen

God's solution is just a prayer away!

Max Lucado

You must go forward on your knees.

Hudson Taylor

No man is greater than his prayer life.

Leonard Ravenhill

Is prayer your steering wheel or your spare tire?

Corrie ten Boom

More from God's Word

In this world you will have trouble.
But take heart! I have overcome the world.
JOHN 16:33 NIV

You, LORD, give true peace to those
who depend on you, because they trust you.
ISAIAH 26:3 NCV

The peace of God, which passeth all understanding,
shall keep your hearts and minds through Christ Jesus.
PHILIPPIANS 4:7 KJV

You will keep in perfect peace those whose minds
are steadfast, because they trust in you.
ISAIAH 26:3 NIV

These things I have spoken to you, that in Me
you may have peace. In the world you will have tribulation;
but be of good cheer, I have overcome the world.
JOHN 16:33 NKJV

A Timely Tip

If you're having troubles of any sort, pray about them. And if you need something, don't ask for God's help in general terms. Ask specifically for the things you need.

75

PRIDE

THE DANGERS OF PRIDE

A patient spirit is better than a proud spirit.
ECCLESIASTES 7:8 HCSB

Dietrich Bonhoeffer observed, "It is very easy to overestimate the importance of our own achievements in comparison with what we owe others." How true. Even those of us who consider ourselves "self-made" men and women are deeply indebted to more people than we can count. Our first and greatest indebtedness, of course, is to God and to His only begotten Son. But we are also indebted to ancestors, parents, teachers, friends, spouses, family members, coworkers, fellow believers…and the list goes on.

With so many people who rightfully deserve to share the credit for our successes, how can we gloat? The answer, of course, is that when we are honest with ourselves, we should never gloat about our accomplishments.

Self-confidence and self-assurance are wonderful traits as long as we keep them in check. But if we allow our feelings of self-importance to obscure our dependence upon God, then we invite His displeasure.

The next time you experience a noteworthy success, remember

this: You are entitled to take pride in your accomplishments, but not too much pride. So instead of puffing out your chest and saying, "Look at me!" give credit where credit is due, starting with God. And remember, too, that there is no such thing as a self-made man or a self-made woman.

All of us are made by God—and He deserves the glory, not us.

MORE THOUGHTS ABOUT PRIDE

Pride builds walls between people,
humility builds bridges.
RICK WARREN

Pride goes before destruction
and a haughty spirit before a fall.
JOSEPH ADDISON

All pride is idolatry.
JOHN WESLEY

If you wish to be miserable,
think much about yourself; about what you want,
what you like, what respect people ought to pay you,
and what people think of you.
CHARLES KINGSLEY

Pride gets no pleasure out of having something,
only out of having more of it than the next man.
C. S. LEWIS

More from God's Word

Do nothing out of rivalry or conceit,
but in humility consider others
as more important than yourselves.
PHILIPPIANS 2:3 HCSB

For those who exalt themselves will be humbled,
and those who humble themselves will be exalted.
MATTHEW 23:12 NIV

You save the humble,
but you bring down those who are proud.
2 SAMUEL 22:28 NCV

When pride comes, disgrace follows,
but with humility comes wisdom.
PROVERBS 11:2 HCSB

God resists the proud,
but gives grace to the humble.
JAMES 4:6 HCSB

A Timely Tip

Remember that humility leads to happiness, and pride doesn't. Max Lucado writes, "God exalts humility. When God works in our lives, helping us to become humble, He gives us a permanent joy. Humility gives us a joy that cannot be taken away." Enough said.

76

PRIORITIES

SETTING THE RIGHT PRIORITIES

*Seek first God's kingdom
and what God wants.
Then all your other needs will be met as well.*
MATTHEW 6:33 NCV

First things first." These words are easy to speak but hard to put into practice. For busy people living in a demanding world, placing first things first can be difficult indeed. Why? Because so many people are expecting so many things from us!

If you're having trouble prioritizing your day, perhaps you've been trying to organize your life according to your own plans, not God's. A better strategy, of course, is to take your daily obligations and place them in the hands of the One who created you. To do so, you must prioritize your day according to God's commandments, and you must seek His will and His wisdom in all matters. Then, you can face the day with the assurance that the same God who created our universe out of nothingness will help you place first things first in your own life.

Do you feel overwhelmed, confused, or emotionally distraught?

Turn the concerns of this day over to God—prayerfully, earnestly, and often. Then, listen for His answer, and trust the answer He gives.

MORE THOUGHTS ABOUT SETTING THE RIGHT PRIORITIES

Great relief and satisfaction can come from seeking God's priorities for us in each season, discerning what is "best" in the midst of many noble opportunities, and pouring our most excellent energies into those things.
BETH MOORE

A disciple is a follower of Christ. That means you take on His priorities as your own. His agenda becomes your agenda. His mission becomes your mission.
CHARLES STANLEY

Energy and time are limited entities. Therefore, we need to use them wisely, focusing on what is truly important.
SARAH YOUNG

Each day is God's gift of a fresh unspoiled opportunity to live according to His priorities.
ELIZABETH GEORGE

Put first things first and we get second things thrown in; put second things first and we lose both first and second things.
ELIZABETH GEORGE

More from God's Word

For where your treasure is,
there your heart will be also.
Luke 12:34 HCSB

Trust in the Lord with all your heart
and lean not on your own understanding.
Proverbs 3:5 NIV

But prove yourselves doers of the word,
and not merely hearers who delude themselves.
James 1:22 NASB

Make yourself an example of good works
with integrity and dignity in your teaching.
Titus 2:7 HCSB

Therefore, whether you eat or drink,
or whatever you do, do everything for God's glory.
1 Corinthians 10:31 HCSB

A Timely Tip

You don't have time to do everything, so it's perfectly okay to say no to the things that mean less so that you'll have time for the things that matter more.

77

PROBLEM SOLVING

PROBLEM SOLVING 101

People who do what is right may have many problems,
but the LORD will solve them all.
PSALM 34:19 NCV

It's inevitable: the upcoming day will not be problem free. In fact, your life can be viewed as an exercise in problem solving. The question is not whether you will encounter difficult people or prickly problems; the real question is how you will choose to respond.

When it comes to solving the problems of everyday living, we often know precisely what needs to be done, but we may be slow in doing it—especially if what needs to be done is difficult or uncomfortable. So we put off till tomorrow what should be done today.

The words of Psalm 34 remind us that the Lord solves problems for "people who do what is right." And usually doing "what is right" means doing the uncomfortable work of confronting our problems sooner rather than later. So with no further ado, let the problem solving begin...now.

More Thoughts about Problem Solving

Every misfortune, every failure,
every loss may be transformed.
God has the power to transform
all misfortunes into "God-sends."
Lettie Cowman

Faith points us beyond our problems
to the hope we have in Christ.
Billy Graham

Human problems are never
greater than divine solutions.
Erwin Lutzer

Each problem is a God-appointed instructor.
Charles Swindoll

Everyone gets discouraged. The question is:
Are you going to give up or get up? It's a choice.
John Maxwell

More from God's Word

I have learned in whatever state I am, to be content.
Philippians 4:11 NKJV

We also have joy with our troubles,
because we know that these troubles
produce patience. And patience produces character,
and character produces hope.
ROMANS 5:3–4 NCV

We are pressured in every way but not crushed;
we are perplexed but not in despair.
2 CORINTHIANS 4:8 HCSB

Trust the LORD your God with all your heart
and lean not on your own understanding;
in all your ways acknowledge him,
and he will make your paths straight.
PROVERBS 3:5–6 NIV

Consider it a great joy, my brothers, whenever you
experience various trials, knowing that
the testing of your faith produces endurance.
But endurance must do its complete work, so that you
may be mature and complete, lacking nothing.
JAMES 1:2–4 HCSB

A TIMELY TIP

There are two kinds of problems that you should never worry about: the small ones that you can handle and the big ones that God can handle. The problems that are simply too big to solve should be left in God's hands while you invest your energy in things that you have the power fix.

78

PROCRASTINATION

BEYOND PROCRASTINATION

But prove yourselves doers of the word,
and not merely hearers who delude themselves.

JAMES 1:22 NASB

If you find yourself bound by the chains of procrastination, ask yourself what you're waiting for—or more accurately what you're afraid of—and why. As you examine the emotional roadblocks that have heretofore blocked your path, you may discover that you're waiting for the "perfect" moment, that instant in time when you feel neither afraid nor anxious. But in truth, perfect moments like these are few and far between.

So stop waiting for the perfect moment and focus, instead, on finding the right moment to do what needs to be done. Then, trust God and get busy. When you do, you'll discover that you and the Father, working together, can accomplish great things...and that you can accomplish them sooner rather than later.

Once you acquire the habit of doing what needs to be done when it needs to be done, you will avoid untold trouble, worry, and stress. So learn to overcome procrastination by paying less attention to your fears and more attention to your responsibilities. God has created a world that punishes procrastinators and rewards people who "do it now." In other words, life doesn't procrastinate. Neither should you.

MORE THOUGHTS ABOUT PROCRASTINATION

Don't wait to "feel" like doing a thing to do it.
Live by decision, not emotion.
JOYCE MEYER

Do noble things, not dream them all day long;
and so make life, death, and that vast forever
one grand, sweet song.
CHARLES KINGSLEY

Our grand business is,
not to see what lies dimly at a distance,
but to do what lies closely at hand.
THOMAS CARLYLE

Every duty which we omit obscures some
truth which we should have known.
JOHN RUSKIN

One today is worth two tomorrows.
BEN FRANKLIN

MORE FROM GOD'S WORD

For the kingdom of God is not a matter of talk but of power.
1 CORINTHIANS 4:20 HCSB

Therefore, with your minds ready for action,
be serious and set your hope completely on the grace
to be brought to you at the revelation of Jesus Christ.
1 PETER 1:13 HCSB

When you make a vow to God, do not delay to fulfill it.
He has no pleasure in fools; fulfill your vow.
ECCLESIASTES 5:4 NIV

People who do what is right may have many problems,
but the LORD will solve them all.
PSALM 34:19 NCV

I can do all things through Him who strengthens me.
PHILIPPIANS 4:13 NASB

A TIMELY TIP

The habit of procrastination is often rooted in the fear of failure, the fear of discomfort, or the fear of embarrassment. Your challenge is to confront these fears and defeat them. So if unpleasant work needs to be done, do it sooner rather than later. It's easy to put off unpleasant tasks, but a far better strategy is this: do the unpleasant work first so you can enjoy the rest of the day. The sooner you face your problems—and the sooner you begin working to resolve them—the better your life will be.

79

PUTTING GOD FIRST

ALWAYS PUT GOD FIRST

You shall have no other gods before Me.
EXODUS 20:3 NKJV

For most of us, these are very busy times. We have obligations at home, at work, at school, or at church. From the moment we rise until we drift off to sleep at night, we have things to do and people to contact. So how do we find time for God? We must *make* time for Him, plain and simple. When we put God first, we're blessed. But when we succumb to the pressures and temptations of the world, we inevitably pay a price for our misguided priorities.

In the book of Exodus, God warns that we should put no gods before Him. Yet all too often, we place our Lord in second, third, or fourth place as we focus on other things. When we place our desires for possessions and status above our love for God—or when we yield to the countless frustrations and distractions that surround us—we forfeit the peace that might otherwise be ours.

In the wilderness, Satan offered Jesus earthly power and unimaginable riches, but Jesus refused. Instead, He chose to worship His heavenly Father. We must do likewise by putting God first and worshiping Him only. God must come first. Always first.

More Thoughts about Putting God First

Jesus Christ is the first and last,
author and finisher, beginning and end,
alpha and omega, and by Him all other
things hold together. He must be first or nothing.
God never comes next!
VANCE HAVNER

God wants to be in our leisure time
as much as He is in our churches and in our work.
BETH MOORE

The most important thing
you must decide to do every day
is put the Lord first.
ELIZABETH GEORGE

Even the most routine part
of your day can be a
spiritual act of worship.
SARAH YOUNG

Christ is either Lord of all,
or He is not Lord at all.
HUDSON TAYLOR

More from God's Word

With my whole heart I have sought You;
oh, let me not wander from Your commandments!
PSALM 119:10 NKJV

Be careful not to forget the LORD.
DEUTERONOMY 6:12 HCSB

Do not love the world or the things that belong to the world.
If anyone loves the world, love for the Father is not in him.
1 JOHN 2:15 HCSB

No one can serve two masters. For you will hate
one and love the other; be devoted to one and despise
the other. You cannot serve God and be enslaved to money.
LUKE 16:13 NLT

Jesus said to him, "'You shall love the LORD your God with
all your heart, with all your soul, and with all your mind.'
This is the first and great commandment."
MATTHEW 22:37–38 NKJV

A Timely Tip

God deserves first place in your heart, and you deserve the experience of putting Him there and keeping Him there. So don't let troublesome circumstances monopolize your thoughts. Put God first. When you do, everything else has a way of falling into place.

80

QUIET TIME

FINDING STRENGTH IN QUIET MOMENTS

In quietness and in confidence shall be your strength.
ISAIAH 30:15 KJV

The world seems to grow louder day by day, and angry people are using technology to spread negativity far and wide. No wonder our senses seem to be invaded at every turn. If we allow difficult people or the distractions of a clamorous society to separate us from God's peace, we do ourselves a profound disservice.

If we sincerely want the peace that passes all understanding, we must carve out time each day for prayer, reflection, and Bible study. When we meet with God in the morning, we can quiet our minds and sense His presence.

Has the busy pace of life robbed you of the peace that God has promised? If so, it's time to reorder your priorities and rearrange your schedule. Nothing is more important than the time you spend with your heavenly Father. So be still and claim the inner peace that is found in the silent moments you spend with Him.

More Thoughts about Quiet Time

*God's voice is still and quiet and easily
buried under an avalanche of clamor.*

CHARLES STANLEY

*The world is full of noise.
Might we not set ourselves to learn silence,
stillness, solitude?*

ELISABETH ELLIOT

*Strength is found not in busyness
and noise but in quietness.*

LETTIE COWMAN

*Nothing in all creation
is so like God as stillness.*

JOHANN WOLFGANG VON GOETHE

*I don't see how any Christian can survive,
let alone live life as more than a conqueror,
apart from a quiet time alone with God.*

KAY ARTHUR

More from God's Word

To every thing there is a season…
a time to keep silence, and a time to speak.
ECCLESIASTES 3:1, 7 KJV

Truly my soul silently waits for God;
from Him comes my salvation.
PSALM 62:1 NKJV

Listen in silence before me.
ISAIAH 41:1 NLT

Be still, and know that I am God.
PSALM 46:10 KJV

Now in the morning,
having risen a long while before daylight,
He went out and departed to a solitary place;
and there He prayed.
MARK 1:35 NKJV

A Timely Tip

You live in a noisy world filled with distractions, interruptions, and occasional frustrations, a world where silence is in short supply. But God wants you carve out quiet moments with Him. Silence is, indeed, golden. Value yours.

81

REGRET

MAKE PEACE WITH YOUR PAST

One thing I do, forgetting those things
which are behind and reaching forward to those things
which are ahead, I press toward the goal for the prize
of the upward call of God in Christ Jesus.

PHILIPPIANS 3:13–14 NKJV

Some of life's greatest emotional roadblocks are not the ones we see through the windshield; they are, instead, the roadblocks that seem to fill the rearview mirror. Because we are imperfect human beings who lack perfect control over our thoughts, we may allow ourselves to become emotionally stuck in the past, even though we know better. Instead of focusing our thoughts and energies on the opportunities of today, we may allow painful memories to fill our minds and sap our strength. We simply can't seem to let go of our pain, so we relive it again and again, with predictably unfortunate consequences. God has other plans.

Philippians 3:13–14 instructs us to focus on the future, not the past. Yet for many of us, focusing on the future is difficult indeed. Why? Part of the problem has to do with forgiveness. When we find ourselves focusing on the past, it's a sure sign that we need to focus, instead, on a more urgent need: the need to forgive. Until we thoroughly and completely forgive those who have hurt us—and until we completely forgive ourselves—we remain stuck.

If you've endured a difficult past, learn from it, mourn it, memorialize it if you must, but don't live in it. Instead, build your future on a firm foundation of trust and forgiveness with no regrets; trust in your heavenly Father and forgiveness for all His children, including yourself. Give all your yesterdays to God, and celebrate this day with hope in your heart and praise on your lips. Your Creator intends to use you in wonderful, unexpected ways if you let Him. But first, God wants you to make peace with your past. And He wants you to do it now.

MORE THOUGHTS ABOUT MAKING PEACE WITH YOUR PAST

Don't be bound by the past and its failures.
But don't forget its lessons either.
BILLY GRAHAM

Don't waste energy regretting the way things are or thinking
about what might have been. Start at the present moment—
accepting things exactly as they are—and search for
My way in the midst of those circumstances.
SARAH YOUNG

Trust the past to God's mercy, the present to God's love,
and the future to God's providence.
ST. AUGUSTINE

MORE FROM GOD'S WORD

And He who sits on the throne said,
"Behold, I am making all things new."
REVELATION 21:5 NASB

Have mercy on me, O God, according to your
unfailing love; according to your great compassion
blot out my transgressions. Wash away all
my iniquity and cleanse me from my sin.
PSALM 51:1–2 NIV

He restoreth my soul: he leadeth me
in the paths of righteousness for his name's sake.
PSALM 23:3 KJV

Your old sinful self has died,
and your new life is kept with Christ in God.
COLOSSIANS 3:3 NCV

Do not remember the former things,
nor consider the things of old.
Behold, I will do a new thing.
ISAIAH 43:18–19 NKJV

A TIMELY TIP

The past is past. Don't invest all your mental energy there. If you're focusing on yesterday, it's time to change your focus. If you're living in the past, move on while there's still time.

82

RENEWAL

HE CAN RESTORE YOUR STRENGTH

You are being renewed in the spirit of your minds;
you put on the new self, the one created according
to God's likeness in righteousness and purity of the truth.
EPHESIANS 4:23–24 HCSB

On occasion, the demands of daily life can drain us of our strength and rob us of the joy that is rightfully ours in Christ. When we find ourselves emotionally drained, discouraged, or worse, there is a source from which we can draw the power needed to recharge our spiritual batteries. That source is God.

When we genuinely lift our hearts and prayers to God, He renews our strength.

Are you troubled or anxious? Take your anxieties to God in prayer. Are you weak or worried? Delve deeply into God's holy Word and sense His presence in the quiet moments of the early morning. Are you spiritually exhausted? Call upon fellow believers to support you, and call upon Christ to renew your spirit and your life. The Lord will never let you down. To the contrary, He will always lift you up if you ask Him to. And the best moment to ask for His help is always the present one.

More Thoughts about Renewal

God is not running an antique shop!
He is making all things new!
VANCE HAVNER

Are you weak? Weary? Confused? Troubled? Pressured?
How is your relationship with God?
Is it held in its place of priority?
I believe the greater the pressure,
the greater your need for time alone with Him.
KAY ARTHUR

God specializes in giving people a fresh start.
RICK WARREN

The creation of a new heart, the renewing
of a right spirit is an omnipotent work of God.
Leave it to the Creator.
HENRY DRUMMOND

Our Lord never drew power from Himself;
He drew it always from His Father.
OSWALD CHAMBERS

More from God's Word

*Now the God of all grace, who called you to
His eternal glory in Christ Jesus, will personally restore,
establish, strengthen, and support you.*
1 Peter 5:10 HCSB

*Those who hope in the Lord will renew their strength.
They will soar on wings like eagles; they will run
and not grow weary, they will walk and not be faint.*
Isaiah 40:31 NIV

*Finally, brothers, rejoice. Become mature, be encouraged,
be of the same mind, be at peace,
and the God of love and peace will be with you.*
2 Corinthians 13:11 HCSB

*Remember ye not the former things, neither consider
the things of old. Behold, I will do a new thing.*
Isaiah 43:18–19 KJV

*Therefore, if anyone is in Christ, he is a new creation; old
things have passed away; behold, all things have become new.*
2 Corinthians 5:17 NKJV

A Timely Tip

God can make all things new, including you. When you are weak or
worried, He can renew your spirit and restore your strength. Your
job, of course, is to let Him.

83

RESPONSIBILITY

TAKING RESPONSIBILITY

But each person should examine his own work,
and then he will have a reason for boasting
in himself alone, and not in respect to someone else.
For each person will have to carry his own load.

GALATIANS 6:4–5 HCSB

God's Word encourages us to take responsibility for our actions, but the world tempts us to do otherwise. The media tries to convince us that we're "victims" of our upbringing, our government, our economic strata, or our circumstances, thus ignoring the countless blessings—and the gift of free will—that the Lord has given each of us.

Who's responsible for your behavior? God's Word says that you are. If you obey His instructions and follow His Son, you'll be blessed in countless ways. But if you ignore the Lord's teachings, you must eventually bear the consequences of those irresponsible decisions.

Self-pity is an emotion that causes far more problems than it solves. Charles Swindoll advises, "When you're on the verge of throwing a pity party thanks to your despairing thoughts, go back to the Word of God." How true. Self-pity is not only an unproductive way to think, it is also an affront to your Father in heaven.

Bitterness and joy cannot coexist in the same heart. Thanksgiving and despair are mutually exclusive. So if your unreliable thoughts are allowing pain and worry to control your emotions and dominate your life, you must train yourself to think less about your troubles and more about God's blessings.

Today and every day, as you make decisions about the things you'll say and do, remember who's responsible. And if you make a mistake, admit it, learn from it, and move on. The blame game has no winners; don't play.

MORE THOUGHTS ON TAKING RESPONSIBILITY

We talk about circumstances that are "beyond our control."
None of us have control over our circumstances,
but we are responsible for the way we
pilot ourselves in the midst of things as they are.
OSWALD CHAMBERS

Action springs not from thought,
but from a readiness for responsibility.
DIETRICH BONHOEFFER

Man must cease attributing his problems
to his environment, and learn again to exercise his will—
his personal responsibility in the realm of faith and morals.
ALBERT SCHWEITZER

More from God's Word

We must do the works of Him
who sent Me while it is day.
Night is coming when no one can work.
John 9:4 HCSB

Better to be patient than powerful;
it is better to have self-control than to conquer a city.
Proverbs 16:32 NLT

By their fruits ye shall know them.
Matthew 7:20 KJV

Then He said to His disciples,
"The harvest is abundant,
but the workers are few."
Matthew 9:37 HCSB

So then, each of us will give
an account of himself to God.
Romans 14:12 HCSB

A Timely Tip

It's easy to hold other people accountable, but real accountability begins with the person you see in the mirror. When you accept responsibility and take steps to resolve your problems, you'll feel better about yourself. So don't look for someone you can blame; look for something constructive that you can do.

84

SAYING NO

YES, YOU HAVE THE RIGHT TO SAY NO

*Let us lay aside every weight, and the sin
which so easily ensnares us, and let us run
with endurance the race that is set before us.*
HEBREWS 12:1 NKJV

If you haven't yet learned to say no—to say it politely, firmly, and often—you're inviting untold stress into your life. Why? Because if you can't say no (when appropriate), some people will take advantage of your good nature.

If you have trouble standing up for yourself, perhaps you're afraid that you'll be rejected. But here's a tip: don't worry too much about rejection, especially when you're rejected for doing the right thing.

Pleasing other people is a good thing up to a point. But you must never allow your "willingness to please" to interfere with your own good judgment or with God's priorities. God gave you a conscience for a reason: to inform you about the things you need to do as well as the things you don't need to do. It's up to you to follow your conscience wherever it may lead, even if it means making unpopular decisions. Your job, simply put, is to be popular with God, not people.

More Thoughts about Saying No

Prescription for a happier and healthier life:
resolve to slow your pace;
learn to say no gracefully;
reject the temptation to chase after
more pleasures, more hobbies,
and more social entanglements.
James Dobson

Efficiency is enhanced not by
what we accomplish but more often
by what we relinquish.
Charles Swindoll

Learn to say "no" to the good
so you can say "yes" to the best.
John Maxwell

As you live your life,
you must localize and define it.
You cannot do everything.
Phillips Brooks

You must learn to say no when
something is not right for you.
Leontyne Price

More from God's Word

Discretion will protect you
and understanding will guard you.
PROVERBS 2:11 NIV

Keep your eyes focused on what is right.
Keep looking straight ahead to what is good.
PROVERBS 4:25 ICB

The fear of man is a snare,
but the one who trusts in the LORD is protected.
PROVERBS 29:25 HCSB

My son, if sinners entice you, don't be persuaded.
PROVERBS 1:10 HCSB

Obviously, I'm not trying to win
the approval of people, but of God.
If pleasing people were my goal, I
would not be Christ's servant.
GALATIANS 1:10 NLT

A Timely Tip

You can't do everything, which means that you need to learn how to say no politely and often. Sometimes people make unreasonable requests, and when they do, you have the right to decline without feeling guilty.

85

SELF-CONFIDENCE

BUILDING SELF-CONFIDENCE

You are my hope; O Lord GOD, You are my confidence.
PSALM 71:5 NASB

Do you believe that you deserve the best, and do you believe that you can achieve the best? Or have you convinced yourself that you're a second-tier talent who'll be lucky to finish far back in the pack? Before you answer these questions, remember this: God sent His Son so that you might enjoy the abundant life that Jesus describes in the familiar words of John 10:10. But God's gifts are not guaranteed—it's up to you to claim them.

If you want to achieve the best that life has to offer, you must put the "self-fulfilling prophecy" to work for you. How? By convincing yourself beyond a shadow of a doubt that you have the ability to earn the rewards you desire. You must become sold on yourself— sold on your skills, sold on your opportunities, sold on your potential, sold on your attitude, and sold on your character. If you're sold on yourself, chances are the world will soon become sold too. And the results will be beautiful.

More Thoughts about Self-Confidence

You need to make the right decision—
firmly and decisively—
and then stick with it, with God's help.
Billy Graham

Never yield to gloomy anticipation.
Lettie Cowman

Confidence in the natural world
is self-reliance; in the spiritual world,
it is God-reliance.
Oswald Chambers

If you doubt you can accomplish something,
you can't accomplish it. Instead,
you have to be confident in yourself
and you need to be tough enough to follow through.
Rosalynn Carter

We need to recognize that lack of confidence
does not equal humility. In fact, genuinely
humble people have enormous confidence
because it rests in a great God.
Beth Moore

MORE FROM GOD'S WORD

So we may boldly say: "The LORD is my helper;
I will not fear. What can man do to me?"
HEBREWS 13:6 NKJV

I lift up my eyes to the mountains—where does my help come from?
My help comes from the LORD, the Maker of heaven and earth.
PSALM 121:1–2 NIV

God is our refuge and strength,
a very present help in trouble.
PSALM 46:1 NKJV

Be strong and courageous, and do the work.
Don't be afraid or discouraged, for the LORD God,
my God, is with you. He won't leave you or forsake you.
1 CHRONICLES 28:20 HCSB

Be on guard. Stand firm in the faith.
Be courageous. Be strong.
1 CORINTHIANS 16:13 NLT

A TIMELY TIP

Don't make the mistake of selling yourself short. No matter the
size of your challenges, you can be sure that you and God, working
together, can handle them. The next time you're tempted to give up
on yourself, remember that God will never, never, never give up on
you. And with God in your corner, you have nothing to fear.

86

SELF-DISCIPLINE

THE POWER OF SELF-DISCIPLINE

For the Spirit God gave us does not
make us timid, but gives us power,
love and self-discipline.
2 TIMOTHY 1:7 NIV

God's Word reminds us again and again that our Creator expects us to lead disciplined lives. God doesn't reward laziness, misbehavior, or apathy. To the contrary, He expects us to behave with dignity and discipline. But ours is a world in which dignity and discipline are often in short supply.

We live in a world in which leisure is glorified and indifference is often glamorized. But God has other plans. God gives us talents, and He expects us to use them. But it is not always easy to cultivate those talents. Sometimes we must invest countless hours (or, in some cases, many years) honing our skills. And that's perfectly okay with God, because He understands that self-discipline is a blessing, not a burden.

Proverbs 23:12 advises: "Apply your heart to discipline and your ears to words of knowledge" (NASB). And 2 Peter 1:5–6 teaches, "Make every effort to supplement your faith with goodness, goodness with knowledge, knowledge with self-control, self-control with endurance, endurance with godliness" (HSCB). Thus, God's Word is clear: we must exercise self-discipline in all matters.

When we pause to consider how much work needs to be done, we realize that self-discipline is not simply a proven way to get ahead, it's also an integral part of God's plan for our lives. If we genuinely seek to be faithful stewards of our time, our talents, and our resources, we must adopt a disciplined approach to life. Otherwise, our talents are wasted and our resources are squandered.

Life's greatest rewards seldom fall into our laps; to the contrary, our greatest accomplishments usually require work, perseverance, and discipline. May we, as disciplined believers, be willing to work for the rewards we so earnestly desire.

MORE THOUGHTS ABOUT
SELF-DISCIPLINE

Pray as though everything depended on God.
Work as though everything depended on you.
ST. AUGUSTINE

There's some task which the God of all the universe,
the great Creator, has for you to do, and which
will remain undone and incomplete, until by faith
and obedience, you step into the will of God.
ALAN REDPATH

The one word in the spiritual vocabulary is now.
OSWALD CHAMBERS

More from God's Word

Well done, good and faithful servant;
you were faithful over a few things, I will make you
ruler over many things. Enter into the joy of your lord.
MATTHEW 25:21 NKJV

For the kingdom of God is not
a matter of talk but of power.
1 CORINTHIANS 4:20 HCSB

When you make a vow to God,
do not delay to fulfill it.
He has no pleasure in fools; fulfill your vow.
ECCLESIASTES 5:4 NIV

Whenever we have the opportunity,
we should do good to everyone—
especially to those in the family of faith.
GALATIANS 6:10 NLT

But prove yourselves doers of the word,
and not merely hearers who delude themselves.
JAMES 1:22 NASB

A Timely Tip

If you're planning on becoming a disciplined person "someday" in the distant future, you're deluding yourself. The best day to begin exercising self-discipline is this one.

87

SELF-EXAMINATION

GETTING TO KNOW YOURSELF

And why worry about a speck in your friend's eye when you have a log in your own? How can you think of saying to your friend, "Let me help you get rid of that speck in your eye," when you can't see past the log in your own eye? Hypocrite! First get rid of the log in your own eye; then you will see well enough to deal with the speck in your friend's eye.

MATTHEW 7:3-5 NLT

If you're looking for better ways to manage your emotions, it's tempting to focus exclusively on the stressors around you. But it's also helpful to look at the stressors within you. Perhaps you're overestimating the size of your problems; perhaps you're being overly pessimistic; perhaps you're being too hard on other people. Or perhaps you have other issues that are stealing your joy day by day and moment by moment.

If you're experiencing hurtful feelings that just won't go away, it's time to schedule an appointment with your pastor or with a pastoral counselor or with a mental health professional. These people can help you look inside to discover, and then banish, the hurtful feelings or exaggerated thought patterns that may be holding you back. When you examine yourself—as you look at your own personal history and your habitual ways of dealing with the world around you—you may decide it's time to make some changes. If so, here's twofold advice: get started now and be patient.

Being patient with other people can be difficult. But sometimes we find it even more difficult to be patient with ourselves. We have high expectations and lofty goals. We want to accomplish things now, not later. And, of course, we want our lives to unfold according to our own timetables, not God's.

Throughout the Bible, we are instructed that patience is the companion of wisdom. God's message, then, is clear: we must be patient with all people, beginning with that particular person who stares back at us each time we gaze into the mirror. So if you happen to be your own worst critic—or if you expect perfection from yourself (not to mention others), it's time to reconsider. When you look inward—and upward—you'll discover that life doesn't have to be perfect to be wonderful.

MORE THOUGHTS ABOUT SELF-EXAMINATION

The man who does not like self-examination may be pretty certain that things need examining.
C. H. SPURGEON

Observe all men, thyself most.
BEN FRANKLIN

The man who has no inner life is the slave to his surroundings.
HENRI-FRÉDÉRIC AMIEL

More from God's Word

*And you shall know the truth,
and the truth shall make you free.*
JOHN 8:32 NKJV

*I urge you who have been chosen by God
to live up to the life to which God called you.*
EPHESIANS 4:1 NCV

*Commit yourself to instruction;
listen carefully to words of knowledge.*
PROVERBS 23:12 NLT

*Let the wise listen and add to their learning,
and let the discerning get guidance.*
PROVERBS 1:5 NIV

*Wisdom is the principal thing; therefore get wisdom.
And in all your getting, get understanding.*
PROVERBS 4:7 NKJV

A Timely Tip

As you journey through life, you should continue to become better aquatinted with yourself. How? One way is to examine the patterns in your own life and understand that unless you make the conscious effort to change those patterns, you're likely to repeat them. So if you don't like some of the results you've earned, change your behaviors. The sooner you change, the sooner your results will change too.

88

SHAME

BEYOND SHAME

Let us come near to God with a sincere heart and a sure faith, because we have been made free from a guilty conscience, and our bodies have been washed with pure water.

HEBREWS 10:22 NCV

Have you done things you're ashamed of? If so, welcome to a very large club. Even the very best people on the planet have done things that only God can forgive. But the good news is this: whenever we admit our shortcomings to God and ask for His forgiveness, He gives it.

There's nothing any of us can do to redeem ourselves from sin; that's something only God can do. So what can we do? We can allow God's Son into our hearts and allow Him to do what we cannot.

Shame is a form of spiritual cancer; it can be deadly, but it is treatable. The treatment begins when we acknowledge our sins and ask for God's mercy. But it doesn't end there. Once God forgives us, we still have work to do: we must forgive ourselves.

God knows all your imperfections, all your faults, and all your shortcomings...and He loves you anyway. And because God loves you, you can—and should—feel good about the person you see when you look into the mirror. God's love is bigger and more powerful than anybody (including you) can imagine, but His love is very real. So do yourself a favor right now: accept God's love with open arms. And while you're at it, remember this: even when you don't love yourself very much, God loves you. And God is always right.

MORE THOUGHTS ABOUT SHAME

The purpose of guilt is to bring us to Jesus.
Once we are there, then its purpose is finished.
If we continue to make ourselves guilty—
to blame ourselves—then that is a sin in itself.
CORRIE TEN BOOM

The most marvelous ingredient in the forgiveness
of God is that He also forgets, the one thing
a human being cannot do. With God,
forgetting is a divine attribute.
God's forgiveness forgets.
OSWALD CHAMBERS

God does not wish us to remember
what He is willing to forget.
GEORGE A. BUTTRICK

If God forgives us and we do not forgive ourselves,
we make ourselves greater than God.
EDWIN LOUIS COLE

More from God's Word

Be gracious to me, God, according to Your faithful love;
according to Your abundant compassion, blot out my rebellion.
Wash away my guilt, and cleanse me from my sin.
PSALM 51:1–2 HCSB

How can I know all the sins lurking in my heart?
Cleanse me from these hidden faults.
Keep your servant from deliberate sins! Don't let them control me.
Then I will be free of guilt and innocent of great sin.
PSALM 19:12–13 NLT

Create in me a pure heart, God,
and make my spirit right again.
PSALM 51:10 NCV

If we confess our sins, He is faithful and righteous
to forgive us our sins and to cleanse us from all unrighteousness.
1 JOHN 1:9 NASB

Guard your heart above all else, for it is the source of life.
PROVERBS 4:23 HCSB

A Timely Tip

If you're being victimized by shame, it's time to have a heart-to-heart talk with your Creator. If you've asked for God's forgiveness, He has given it. And because He has forgiven you, you should be quick to forgive yourself and make peace with your past. To do otherwise is to hold yourself to a different standard than God does.

89

SPEECH

CHOOSE YOUR WORDS CAREFULLY

Let the words of my mouth and the meditation
of my heart be acceptable in Your sight,
O LORD, my strength and my Redeemer.
PSALM 19:14 NKJV

The words that we speak have great power. If our words are encouraging, we can lift others up; if our words are hurtful, we can hold others back. The Bible reminds us that "words of the reckless pierce like swords, but the tongue of the wise brings healing" (Proverbs 12:18 NIV). Therefore, if we are to solve more problems than we start, we must measure our words carefully.

Sometimes even the most thoughtful among us speak first and think second (with decidedly mixed results). When we're frustrated or tired, we may speak words that would be better left unspoken. Whenever we lash out in anger, we forgo the wonderful opportunity to consider our thoughts before we give voice to them.

A far better strategy, of course, is to do the more difficult thing: to think first and to speak next. When we do so, we give ourselves ample time to compose our thoughts and to consult our Creator (but not necessarily in that order!).

The Bible warns us that we will be judged by the words we speak (Matthew 12:36–37). And Ephesians 4:29 reminds us that we can—and should—make "each word a gift" (MSG). To do otherwise is to invite God's displeasure.

Do you seek to be a source of encouragement to others? Are you a beacon of hope to your friends and family? And do you seek to be a worthy ambassador for Christ? If so, you must speak words that are worthy of Him. So avoid angry outbursts. Refrain from impulsive outpourings. Terminate tantrums. Instead, speak words of encouragement and hope to a world that desperately needs both.

MORE THOUGHTS ABOUT CHOOSING THE RIGHT WORDS

A little kindly advice is better than a great deal of scolding.
FANNY CROSBY

There are tones of voice that mean more than words.
ROBERT FROST

An able man shows his spirit
by gentle words and resolute actions.
G. K. CHESTERTON

Change the heart, and you change the speech.
WARREN WIERSBE

Talk happiness. The world is sad enough without your woes.
ELLA WHEELER WILCOX

More from God's Word

*Therefore encourage one another
and build each other up as you are already doing.*
1 Thessalonians 5:11 HCSB

*A word spoken at the right time
is like gold apples on a silver tray.*
Proverbs 25:11 HCSB

*But encourage one another day after day,
as long as it is still called "Today," so that none of you
will be hardened by the deceitfulness of sin.*
Hebrews 3:13 NASB

*Now finally, all of you should be
like-minded and sympathetic,
should love believers,
and be compassionate and humble.*
1 Peter 3:8 HCSB

A Timely Tip

When you're not sure what to say, it's perfectly okay to keep your mouth tightly closed. If you find yourself in a highly charged conversation, it's always better to think carefully before you speak. And it's better to say nothing than to say something that fans the flames of anger. Rather than engage in a lengthy disagreement (that will ultimately go nowhere), it's probably better to call time out and leave the scene of the argument.

90

SPIRITUAL GROWTH

SPIRITUAL GROWTH IS ALWAYS POSSIBLE

I remind you to fan into flames the spiritual gift God gave you.
2 TIMOTHY 1:6 NLT

When we cease to grow, either emotionally or spiritually, we do ourselves a profound disservice. But if we study God's Word, if we obey His commandments, and if we live in the center of His will, we will not be "stagnant" believers; we will, instead, be growing Christians, and that's exactly what God wants for our lives and our relationships.

Many of life's most important lessons are painful to learn. Thankfully, during times of heartbreak and hardship, God stands ready to protect us. As Psalm 46:1 promises, "God is our protection and our strength. He always helps in times of trouble" (NCV). In His own time and according to His master plan, God will heal us if we invite Him into our hearts.

Spiritual growth need not take place only in times of adversity. We must seek to grow in our knowledge and love of the Lord every day that we live. Every day is a new opportunity to live, to love, to serve, and to grow.

More Thoughts about Spiritual Growth

God will help us become the people
we are meant to be,
if only we will ask Him.
Hannah Whitall Smith

The vigor of our spiritual life
will be in exact proportion to the place
held by the Bible in our life and thoughts.
George Mueller

Grow, dear friends, but grow,
I beseech you, in God's way,
which is the only true way.
Hannah Whitall Smith

Mark it down.
You will never go where God is not.
Max Lucado

God's ultimate goal for your life on earth
is not comfort, but character development.
He wants you to grow up spiritually
and become like Christ.
Rick Warren

More from God's Word

*So let us stop going over the basic teachings about Christ
again and again. Let us go on instead
and become mature in our understanding.*
HEBREWS 6:1 NLT

*But grow in the grace and knowledge of our Lord and Savior
Jesus Christ. To Him be the glory both now and forever. Amen.*
2 PETER 3:18 NKJV

*Leave inexperience behind, and you will live;
pursue the way of understanding.*
PROVERBS 9:6 HCSB

*And be not conformed to this world:
but be ye transformed by the renewing of your mind,
that ye may prove what is that good,
and acceptable, and perfect will of God.*
ROMANS 12:2 KJV

*But endurance must do its complete work,
so that you may be mature and complete, lacking nothing.*
JAMES 1:4 HCSB

A Timely Tip

When it comes to your faith, God doesn't want you to stand still.
He wants you to keep growing. He knows that spiritual maturity is
a journey, not a destination. You should know it too.

91

STARTING OVER

IF YOU'RE STARTING OVER

Then the One seated on the throne said,
"Look! I am making everything new."
REVELATION 21:5 HCSB

If you've recently extricated yourself from a difficult situation—or if you've been forced to cut ties with someone whose personality was simply too problematic to endure—you may feel like you're entering a new phase of life. If so, congratulations! Your fresh start is an occasion to be celebrated. God has a perfect plan for your life, and He has the power to make all things new.

As you think about your future—and as you consider the countless opportunities that will be woven into the fabric of the days ahead—be sure to include God in your plans. When you do, He will guide your steps and light your path.

Perhaps you desire to change the direction of your life, or perhaps you're determined to make major modifications in the way you live or the way you think. If so, you and God, working together, can do it. But don't expect change to be easy or instant. God expects you to do your fair share of the work, and that's as it should be.

If you're going through a spiritual growth spurt, don't be surprised if you experience a few spiritual growing pains. Why? Because real transformation begins on the inside and works its way out from there. And sometimes the "working out" is painful. Lasting change doesn't occur "out there"; it occurs "in here." It occurs, not in the shifting sands of your own particular circumstances, but in the quiet depths of your own obedient heart. So if you're in search of a new beginning or, for that matter, a new you, don't expect changing circumstances to miraculously transform you into the person you want to become. Transformation starts with God, and it starts in the silent center of a humble human heart—like yours.

MORE THOUGHTS ABOUT STARTING OVER

What saves a man is to take a step.
Then another step.
C. S. LEWIS

The best preparation for the future
is the present well seen to, and the last duty done.
GEORGE MACDONALD

God specializes in giving people a fresh start.
RICK WARREN

Are you in earnest? Seize this very minute.
What you can do, or dream you can, begin it.
Boldness has genius, power, and magic in it.
JOHANN WOLFGANG VON GOETHE

More from God's Word

"For I know the plans I have for you"—
this is the Lord's declaration—plans for your welfare,
not for disaster, to give you a future and a hope."
JEREMIAH 29:11 HCSB

There is one thing I always do. Forgetting the past
and straining toward what is ahead, I keep trying to reach
the goal and get the prize for which God called me.
PHILIPPIANS 3:13–14 NCV

You are being renewed in the spirit of your minds;
you put on the new self, the one created according to God's
likeness in righteousness and purity of the truth.
EPHESIANS 4:23–24 HCSB

Do not remember the former things, nor consider
the things of old. Behold, I will do a new thing.
ISAIAH 43:18–19 NKJV

A Timely Tip

Sometimes, despite our best efforts, relationships must end, and we must move on. If you're enduring the pain of a recent breakup—or living with painful memories of an old relationship gone bad—remember that God has the power to make all things new, including you. So if you're graduating into a new phase of life, be sure to make God your partner. If you do, He'll guide your steps; He'll help carry your burdens; and He'll help you focus on the opportunities of the future, not the losses of the past.

92

STRENGTH

FINDING STRENGTH
TO MANAGE YOUR EMOTIONS

He gives strength to the weary,
and to him who lacks might He increases power.
ISAIAH 40:29 NASB

God's love and support never change. From the cradle to the grave, God has promised to give you the strength to meet any challenge. God has promised to lift you up and guide your steps if you let Him. God has promised that when you entrust your life to Him completely and without reservation, He will give you the courage to face any trial and the wisdom to live in His righteousness.

Are you an energized Christian? You should be. But if you're not, you must seek emotional strength from the source that will never fail: that source, of course, is your heavenly Father. And rest assured—when you sincerely petition Him, He will give you all the strength you need to live victoriously for Him.

God has promised to protect us, and He intends to keep His promise. In a world filled with dangers and temptations, God is the ultimate armor. In a world filled with misleading messages, God's Word is the ultimate truth. In a world filled with more frustrations than we can count, God's Son offers the ultimate peace.

More Thoughts on God's Strength

God is in control. He may not
take away trials or make detours for us,
but He strengthens us through them.
BILLY GRAHAM

God will give us the strength
and resources we need to live through
any situation in life that He ordains.
BILLY GRAHAM

Faith is a strong power,
mastering any difficulty in the strength
of the Lord who made heaven and earth.
CORRIE TEN BOOM

The truth is, God's strength is fully revealed
when our strength is depleted.
LIZ CURTIS HIGGS

The strength that we claim from
God's Word does not depend on circumstances.
Circumstances will be difficult,
but our strength will be sufficient.
CORRIE TEN BOOM

More from God's Word

I can do all things through Christ who strengthens me.
PHILIPPIANS 4:13 NKJV

My grace is sufficient for you,
for my power is made perfect in weakness.
2 CORINTHIANS 12:9 NIV

Be strong and courageous, and do the work.
Don't be afraid or discouraged, for the LORD God,
my God, is with you. He won't leave you or forsake you.
1 CHRONICLES 28:20 HCSB

Have faith in the LORD your God,
and you will stand strong. Have faith
in his prophets, and you will succeed.
2 CHRONICLES 20:20 NCV

The LORD is my strength and my song;
He has become my salvation.
EXODUS 15:2 HCSB

A Timely Tip

Need strength? Slow down, get more rest, engage in regular, sensible exercise, and turn your troubles over to God...but not necessarily in that order.

93

STRESS

MANAGING STRESS

*Come unto me, all ye that labor
and are heavy laden, and I will give you rest.*
MATTHEW 11:28 KJV

Stressful days are an inevitable fact of modern life. And how do we best cope with the challenges of our demanding twenty-first-century world? By turning our days and our lives over to God. Elisabeth Elliot wrote, "If my life is surrendered to God, all is well. Let me not grab it back, as though it were in peril in His hand but would be safer in mine!" Yet even the most devout Christians may, at times, seek to grab the reins and proclaim, "I'm in charge!" To do so is foolish, prideful, and stress-inducing.

When we seek to impose our own wills upon the world—or upon other people—we invite stress into our lives...needlessly. But when we turn our lives and our hearts over to God—when we accept His will instead of seeking vainly to impose our own—we discover the inner peace that can be ours through Him.

Do you feel overwhelmed by the stresses of daily life? Turn your concerns and your prayers over to God. Trust Him. Trust Him completely. Trust Him today. Trust Him always. Whatever your concerns, whatever your challenges, hand them over to God completely and without reservation. He knows your needs and will meet those needs in His own way and in His own time if you let Him. He's always with you, always in your corner, always ready to help. And the rest, of course, is up to you.

MORE THOUGHTS ABOUT MANAGING STRESS

There are many burned-out people
who think more is always better,
who deem it unspiritual to say no.
SARAH YOUNG

God specializes in giving people a fresh start.
RICK WARREN

Life is strenuous. See that your clock does not run down.
LETTIE COWMAN

Beware of having so much to do
that you really do nothing at all
because you do not wait upon God to do it aright.
C. H. SPURGEON

The more comfortable we are
with mystery in our journey,
the more rest we will know along the way.
JOHN ELDREDGE

More from God's Word

Live peaceful and quiet lives
in all godliness and holiness.
1 Timothy 2:2 NIV

I find rest in God; only he gives me hope.
Psalm 62:5 NCV

You, Lord, give true peace to those
who depend on you, because they trust you.
Isaiah 26:3 NCV

Peace I leave with you;
My peace I give to you;
not as the world gives do I give to you.
Do not let your heart be troubled,
nor let it be fearful.
John 14:27 NASB

And the peace of God,
which transcends all understanding,
will guard your hearts and your minds in Christ Jesus.
Philippians 4:7 NIV

A Timely Tip

If you're serious about beating stress, then you must form the habit of talking to God first thing every morning. He's available. Are you?

94

SUFFERING AND PAIN

WHEN YOU'RE SUFFERING

*And the God of all grace, who called you to his eternal glory
in Christ, after you have suffered a little while, will himself
restore you and make you strong, firm and steadfast.*
1 PETER 5:10 NIV

All of us face times of adversity. When we face the inevitable difficulties of life here on earth, we can seek help from family, from friends, and from God...but not necessarily in that order.

Barbara Johnson writes, "There is no way around suffering. We have to go through it to get to the other side." And the best way "to get to the other side" of suffering is to get there with God. When we turn open hearts to Him in heartfelt prayer, He will answer—in His own time and according to His own plan—and He will heal us.

And while we are waiting for God's plans to unfold and for His healing touch to restore us, we can be comforted in the knowledge that our Creator can overcome any obstacle, even if we cannot. The Psalmist writes, "Weeping may endure for a night, but joy comes in the morning" (Psalm 30:5 NKJV). But when we are suffering, the morning may seem very far away. It is not. God promises that He is "near to those who have a broken heart" (Psalm 34:18 NKJV).

If you are experiencing the intense pain of a recent loss, or if you are still mourning a loss from long ago, perhaps you are now ready to begin the next stage of your journey with God. If so, be mindful of this fact: the loving heart of God is sufficient to meet any challenge, including yours.

MORE THOUGHTS ABOUT SUFFERING AND PAIN

The promises of God's Word sustain us
in our suffering, and we know Jesus sympathizes
and empathizes with us in our darkest hour.
BILL BRIGHT

God is sufficient for all our needs, for every problem, for every
difficulty, for every broken heart, for every human sorrow.
PETER MARSHALL

You don't have to be alone in your hurt! Comfort is yours.
Joy is an option. And it's all been made possible by your Savior.
JONI EARECKSON TADA

Suffering is never for nothing. It is that you
and I might be conformed to the image of Christ.
ELISABETH ELLIOT

God whispers to us in our pleasures, speaks in our conscience,
but shouts in our pains: it is His megaphone to rouse a deaf world.
C. S. LEWIS

More from God's Word

I have heard your prayer; I have seen your tears.
Look, I will heal you.
2 Kings 20:5 HCSB

I have told you these things so that in Me
you may have peace. You will have suffering in this world.
Be courageous! I have conquered the world.
John 16:33 HCSB

In my distress I called upon the Lord,
and cried unto my God: he heard my voice.
Psalm 18:6 KJV

You who are now hungry are blessed,
because you will be filled.
You who now weep are blessed,
because you will laugh.
Luke 6:21 HCSB

Is anyone among you suffering? He should pray.
James 5:13 HCSB

A Timely Tip

All of us must, from time to time, endure unfortunate circumstances that test our faith. No man or woman, no matter how righteous, is exempt. Christians, however, face their grief with the ultimate armor: God's promises. God will help heal us if we welcome Him into our hearts.

95

TEMPTATION

AVOIDING TEMPTATION

Do not be misled: "Bad company corrupts good character."
1 CORINTHIANS 15:33 NIV

Because our world is filled with temptations, we confront them at every turn. Some of these temptations are small: eating a second piece of chocolate cake, for example. Too much cake may cause us to defile, at least in a modest way, the bodily temple that God has entrusted to our care. But two pieces of cake will not bring us to our knees. Other temptations, however, are not so harmless.

The devil, it seems, is working overtime these days, and causing heartache in more places and in more ways than ever before. We, as Christians, must remain vigilant. Not only must we resist Satan when he confronts us, but we must also avoid those places where Satan can most easily tempt us. And if we are to avoid the unending temptations of this world, we must arm ourselves with the Word of God.

In a letter to believers, Peter offered a stern warning: "Be sober, be vigilant; because your adversary the devil walks about like a roaring lion, seeking whom he may devour" (1 Peter 5:8 NKJV). What was true in New Testament times is equally true in our own. Satan tempts his prey and then devours them. And in these dangerous times, the tools that Satan uses to destroy his prey are more numerous than ever before.

After fasting forty days and nights in the desert, Jesus Himself was tempted by Satan. Christ used Scripture to rebuke the devil (Matthew 4:1–11). We must do likewise. The Holy Bible provides us with a perfect blueprint for righteous living. If we consult that blueprint each day and follow its instructions carefully, we build our lives according to God's plan. And when we do, we are secure.

More Thoughts about Temptation

Every temptation, directly or indirectly,
is the temptation to doubt and distrust God.
John MacArthur

It is not the temptations you have,
but the decision you make about them, that counts.
Billy Graham

Temptations that have been anticipated,
guarded against, and prayed about have little power
to harm us. Jesus tells us to "keep watching and praying,
that you may not come into temptation."
John MacArthur

The first step on the way to victory is to recognize the enemy.
Corrie ten Boom

More from God's Word

Let us lay aside every weight, and the sin
which so easily ensnares us, and let us run
with endurance the race that is set before us.
HEBREWS 12:1 NKJV

Test all things; hold fast what is good.
Abstain from every form of evil.
1 THESSALONIANS 5:21–22 NKJV

But encourage each other daily, while it is still called today,
so that none of you is hardened by sin's deception.
HEBREWS 3:13 HCSB

Put on the whole armor of God, that you may
be able to stand against the wiles of the devil.
EPHESIANS 6:11 NKJV

No temptation has overtaken you but such as is
common to man; and God is faithful, who will not
allow you to be tempted beyond what you are able,
but with the temptation will provide the way of escape.
1 CORINTHIANS 10:13 NASB

A Timely Tip

It's an old saying and a true one: "When it comes to temptation, it's easier to stay out than it is to get out."

96

THOUGHTS

GUARD YOUR THOUGHTS

Finally, brothers and sisters, whatever is true, whatever is noble,
whatever is right, whatever is pure, whatever is lovely,
whatever is admirable—if anything is excellent
or praiseworthy—think about such things.

PHILIPPIANS 4:8 NIV

How will you direct your thoughts today? Will you obey the words of Philippians 4:8 by dwelling upon those things that are noble, pure, and admirable? Or will you allow your thoughts to be hijacked by difficult people or by the general negativity that seems to dominate our troubled world?

Are you fearful, angry, frustrated, or worried? Are you so preoccupied with the concerns of this day that you fail to thank God for the promise of eternity? Are you confused, bitter, or pessimistic? If so, God wants to have a little talk with you.

God intends that you be an ambassador for Him, an enthusiastic, hope-filled Christian. But God won't force you to adopt a positive attitude. It's up to you to think positively about your blessings and your opportunities. When you do so, your positive thoughts will generate positive emotions.

So today and every day hereafter, celebrate this life that God has given you by focusing your thoughts and your energies upon things that are excellent and praiseworthy. It's the best way to think and the best way to live.

MORE THOUGHTS ABOUT GUARDING YOUR THOUGHTS

Change always starts in your mind.
The way you think determines the way you feel,
and the way you feel influences the way you act.
RICK WARREN

When you think on the powerful truths of Scripture,
God uses His Word to change your way of thinking.
ELIZABETH GEORGE

It is the thoughts and intents of the heart
that shape a person's life.
JOHN ELDREDGE

The things we think are the things that feed our souls.
If we think on pure and lovely things, we shall grow pure
and lovely like them; and the converse is equally true.
HANNAH WHITALL SMITH

Your life today is a result of your thinking yesterday.
Your life tomorrow will be determined by what you think today.
JOHN MAXWELL

More from God's Word

For to be carnally minded is death,
but to be spiritually minded is life and peace.
ROMANS 8:6 NKJV

The peace of God, which surpasses all understanding,
will guard your hearts and minds through Christ Jesus.
PHILIPPIANS 4:7 NKJV

And do not be conformed to this world,
but be transformed by the renewing of your mind,
so that you may prove what the will of God is,
that which is good and acceptable and perfect.
ROMANS 12:2 NASB

Guard your heart above all else,
for it is the source of life.
PROVERBS 4:23 HCSB

Set your mind on things above,
not on things on the earth.
COLOSSIANS 3:2 NKJV

A Timely Tip

Sometimes negative thoughts can hijack your emotions. If that happens to you, slow down and try to reconnect with reality. Here are the facts: God's love is real; His peace is real; His support is real. Don't ever let your emotions obscure these truths.

97

TODAY

TODAY IS A GIFT

*So teach us to number our days,
that we may present to You a heart of wisdom.*
PSALM 90:12 NASB

This day is a blessed gift from God. And as Christians, we have countless reasons to rejoice. Yet on some days, when encounters with difficult people or the demands of difficult circumstances threaten to overwhelm us, we don't feel much like rejoicing. Instead of celebrating God's glorious creation, we hit emotional speed bumps that leave us frustrated, discouraged, worried, or anxious.

The familiar words of Psalm 118:24 remind us that "this is the day which the Lord hath made; we will rejoice and be glad in it" (KJV). So whatever this day holds for you, begin it and end it with God as your partner. And throughout the day, give thanks to the One who created you. God's love for you is infinite. Accept it joyfully. And be thankful.

The gift of time is, indeed, a gift from above. Treat it as if it were a precious, fleeting, one-of-a-kind treasure. Because it is.

More Thoughts about the Gift of Today

The one word in the spiritual vocabulary is now.
Oswald Chambers

Each day is God's gift
of a fresh unspoiled opportunity
to live according to His priorities.
Elizabeth George

Yesterday is the tomb of time,
and tomorrow is the womb of time.
Only now is yours.
R. G. Lee

Today is mine. Tomorrow is none of my business.
If I peer anxiously into the fog of the future,
I will strain my spiritual eyes so that
I will not see clearly what is required of me now.
Elisabeth Elliot

Faith does not concern itself with the entire journey.
One step is enough.
Lettie Cowman

More from God's Word

These things I have spoken to you,
that My joy may remain in you,
and that your joy may be full.
JOHN 15:11 NKJV

So don't worry about tomorrow,
because tomorrow will have its own worries.
Each day has enough trouble of its own.
MATTHEW 6:34 NCV

But encourage each other every day while it is "today."
Help each other so none of you will become
hardened because sin has tricked you.
HEBREWS 3:13 NCV

The world and its desires pass away,
but whoever does the will of God lives forever.
1 JOHN 2:17 NIV

There is a time for everything,
and a season for every activity under the heavens.
ECCLESIASTES 3:1 NIV

A Timely Tip

Every day is a beautifully wrapped gift from the Lord. Unwrap it, use it wisely, and give thanks to the Giver.

98

UNDERSTANDING

PRAY FOR AN UNDERSTANDING HEART

Teach me, O LORD, the way of Your statutes,
and I shall keep it to the end.
PSALM 119:33 NKJV

What a blessing it is when our friends and loved ones genuinely seek to understand who we are and what we think. Just as we seek to be understood by others, so, too, should we seek to understand the hopes and dreams of our family members and friends.

We live in a busy world populated by fallible people who misbehave from time to time. When we're frustrated or upset by their behavior, it is all too easy to overlook their needs and motivations. But God's Word instructs us to do otherwise. In the Gospel of Matthew, Jesus declared, "In everything, therefore, treat people the same way you want them to treat you, for this is the Law and the Prophets" (Matthew 7:12 NASB).

Today, as you consider all the things that Christ has done in you, honor Him by being a little kinder than necessary. Honor Christ by slowing down long enough to notice the trials and tribulations of your neighbors. Honor Christ by giving the gift of understanding to friends and to family members alike, even when they fall short of your expectations. As a believer who has been eternally blessed by a loving Savior, you should do no less.

MORE THOUGHTS ABOUT HAVING AN UNDERSTANDING HEART

If we neglect the Bible,
we cannot expect to benefit from
the wisdom and direction that result
from knowing God's Word.
VONETTE BRIGHT

Make it the first morning business
of your life to understand some part
of the Bible clearly, and make it
your daily business to obey it.
JOHN RUSKIN

The only way we can understand the Bible
is by personal contact with the Living Word.
OSWALD CHAMBERS

God will see to it that we understand
as much truth as we are willing to obey.
ELISABETH ELLIOT

Get into the habit of dealing
with God about everything.
OSWALD CHAMBERS

More from God's Word

Who among you is wise and understanding?
Let him show by his good behavior
his deeds in the gentleness of wisdom.
James 3:13 NASB

A foolish person enjoys doing wrong, but a person
with understanding enjoys doing what is wise.
Proverbs 10:23 NCV

Wisdom and strength belong to God;
counsel and understanding are His.
Job 12:13 HCSB

A wise man will hear, and will increase learning;
and a man of understanding shall attain unto wise counsels.
Proverbs 1:5 KJV

Morning by morning he wakens me and opens
my understanding to his will. The Sovereign LORD
has spoken to me, and I have listened.
Isaiah 50:4–5 NLT

A Timely Tip

If you're trying to solve a difficult problem—or if you're dealing with a difficult person—you need wisdom: God's wisdom. Be thankful that the Lord always makes His wisdom available to you. Your job is to acknowledge it, to understand it, and to apply it.

99

WISDOM

TRUST GOD'S WISDOM

*For the LORD gives wisdom; from His mouth
come knowledge and understanding.*
PROVERBS 2:6 HCSB

Real wisdom doesn't come from talk radio, reality TV, the sports page, the evening news, or a Facebook page. In fact, searching for genuine nuggets of wisdom in the endless stream of modern-day media messages is like panning for gold without a pan—only harder. Why? Because real wisdom doesn't come from the world; it comes from God...and it's up to you to ask Him for it: "Ask, and it will be given to you; seek, and you will find; knock, and it will be opened to you. For everyone who asks receives, and he who seeks finds, and to him who knocks it will be opened" (Matthew 7:7–8 NKJV). Jesus made it clear to His disciples that they should petition God to meet their needs. So should you.

Genuine, heartfelt prayer produces powerful changes in you and in your world. When you lift your heart to God, you open yourself to a never-ending source of divine wisdom and infinite love. Yet too many folks are too timid or too pessimistic to ask God for help. Please don't count yourself among their number.

God will give you wisdom if you have the courage to ask Him (and the determination to keep asking Him). If you call upon Him, He will give you guidance and perspective. If you make God's priorities your priorities, He will lead you along a path of His choosing. If you study God's teachings, you will be reminded that God's reality is the ultimate reality.

As you accumulate wisdom, you may feel the need to share your insights with friends and family members. If so, remember this: your actions must reflect the values that you hold dear. The best way to share your wisdom—perhaps the only way—is not by your words, but by your example.

MORE THOUGHTS ABOUT GOD'S WISDOM

Wisdom is the power to see and the inclination to choose the best and highest goal, together with the surest means of attaining it.
J. I. PACKER

Wisdom is the right use of knowledge. To know is not to be wise. There is no fool so great as the knowing fool. But, to know how to use knowledge is to have wisdom.
C. H. SPURGEON

True wisdom is marked by willingness to listen and a sense of knowing when to yield.
ELIZABETH GEORGE

More from God's Word

Who among you is wise and understanding? Let him show
by his good behavior his deeds in the gentleness of wisdom.
JAMES 3:13 NASB

But the wisdom that is from above is first pure,
then peaceable, gentle, willing to yield, full of mercy
and good fruits, without partiality and without hypocrisy.
JAMES 3:17 NKJV

But if any of you lacks wisdom, let him ask of God,
who gives to all generously and without reproach,
and it will be given to him.
JAMES 1:5 NASB

He that walketh with wise men shall be wise:
but a companion of fools shall be destroyed.
PROVERBS 13:20 KJV

Get wisdom—how much better it is than gold!
And get understanding—it is preferable to silver.
PROVERBS 16:16 HCSB

A Timely Tip

Need wisdom? God's got it and He wants you to acquire it. If you want the same thing, then study His Word and associate with godly people.

100

WORRY

TAKE YOUR WORRIES TO GOD, AND LEAVE THEM THERE

Therefore do not worry about tomorrow,
for tomorrow will worry about its own things.
Sufficient for the day is its own trouble.
MATTHEW 6:34 NKJV

Because we are fallible human beings struggling through the inevitable challenges of life here on earth, we worry. Even though we, as Christians, have been promised the gift of eternal life—even though we are blessed by God's love and protection—we find ourselves fretting over the inevitable frustrations of everyday life.

Where is the best place to take your worries? Take them to God. Take your concerns to Him; take your fears to Him; take your doubts to Him; take your weaknesses to Him; take your sorrows to Him…and leave them all there. Seek protection from the Creator and build your spiritual house upon the Rock that cannot be moved. Remind yourself that God still sits in His heaven and that you are His beloved child. Then, perhaps, you will worry less and trust Him more. And that's as it should be because the Lord is trustworthy, and you are protected.

Perhaps you are concerned about your future, your relationships, or your finances. Or perhaps you are simply a "worrier" by nature. If so, choose to make Matthew 6:34 a regular part of your daily Bible reading. This beautiful verse will remind you to live in day-tight compartments and to leave everything else up to God.

MORE THOUGHTS ABOUT WORRY

*Knowing that God is faithful really helps me
to not be captivated by worry.*
JOSH MCDOWELL

Pray, and let God worry.
MARTIN LUTHER

*Worry is the senseless process of cluttering up tomorrow's
opportunities with leftover problems from today.*
BARBARA JOHNSON

*Worry is a cycle of inefficient thoughts
whirling around a center of fear.*
CORRIE TEN BOOM

Too many people worry, but don't do anything about it.
PEARL BAILEY

*Do not worry about tomorrow.
This is not a suggestion, but a command.*
SARAH YOUNG

MORE FROM GOD'S WORD

Cast your burden on the LORD, and He shall sustain you;
He shall never permit the righteous to be moved.
PSALM 55:22 NKJV

Let not your heart be troubled;
you believe in God, believe also in Me.
JOHN 14:1 NKJV

Do not be anxious about anything, but in everything, by prayer
and petition, with thanksgiving, present your requests to God.
PHILIPPIANS 4:6 NIV

Peace I leave with you; My peace I give to you;
not as the world gives do I give to you.
Do not let your heart be troubled, nor let it be fearful.
JOHN 14:27 NASB

Trust the LORD your God with all your heart and lean not
on your own understanding; in all your ways submit to him,
and he will make your paths straight.
PROVERBS 3:5–6 NIV

A TIMELY TIP

Divide your areas of concern into two categories: those you can control and those you can't. Focus on the former and refuse to waste time or energy worrying about the latter. You have worries, but God has solutions. Your challenge it to trust Him to solve the problems that are simply too big for you to resolve on your own.

RECOGNIZING
COMMON MOOD AND
ANXIETY DISORDERS

COMMON MOOD
AND ANXIETY DISORDERS

A mood disorder is a mental health condition that has an adverse effect on a person's emotional state. The two most common mood disorders are depression and bipolar disorder. Both of these conditions are further divided into subcategories based, in part, on the severity and duration of the person's symptoms.

An anxiety disorder is a condition that causes exaggerated emotions to interfere with a person's ability to lead a normal life. All of us feel anxious from time to time, but a person who experiences an anxiety disorder is faced with overwhelming, debilitating feelings of fear, dread, or panic. Obsessive behaviors—characterized by recurrent, unwanted thoughts (obsessions) or undesirable repetitive behaviors (compulsions)—are also considered to be anxiety-related conditions.

Mood and anxiety disorders are quite common. The National Institute of Mental Health (NIMH) estimates that almost 10 percent of US adults will experience a mood disorder during a given year, and that over 20 percent of adults will experience a mood disorder sometime during their lifetime.

Anxiety disorders are even more common than mood disorders. In fact, the NIMH calls anxiety disorders "the most common mental health concern in the United States." They estimate that currently about 40 million adults (almost 20 percent of the adult population) suffer from some type of anxiety-related condition. Common anxiety disorders include, but are not limited to, generalized anxiety disorder, obsessive-compulsive disorder, panic disorder, post-traumatic stress disorder, and social anxiety disorder.

Both mood and anxiety disorders tend to run in families, which means that they can be inherited from one or both parents. Additionally, environmental factors—such as a traumatic event, a serious illness, or a significant life-changing situation—can be causal factors.

Clearly mood and anxiety disorders pose serious problems for individual sufferers and for the loved ones who care for them. Thankfully, these disorders are, in most cases, readily treatable with therapy or medication—or a combination of the two—combined with self-care.

The following descriptions provide a brief introduction to the above-mentioned disorders. Should you need to learn more, detailed information is readily available. And if you suspect that you or someone you care about may be impacted by one of these disorders, or by a mental illness not mentioned here, don't wait to seek treatment. Mental health problems can evolve into serious, debilitating, life-threatening conditions. So it's always better to seek professional guidance sooner rather than later.

THE MOST COMMON MOOD DISORDERS

Major Depression (also known as Major Depressive Disorder or Clinical Depression): Major depression is a common, serious mood disorder. It causes severe symptoms that affect how one feels, thinks, and manages daily activities such as sleeping, eating, or working. To be diagnosed with depression, symptoms must be present for at least two weeks. Symptoms include, but are not limited to, the following:

- Feelings of sadness, hopeless, or despondency
- Feelings of guilt, worthlessness, or helplessness

- Difficulty sleeping, early-morning awakening, or oversleeping
- Having noticeably less interest in usually pleasurable activities
- Decreased energy level
- Appetite or weight changes
- Feeling that life no longer has meaning
- Irritability
- Moving or talking more slowly
- Feeling restless or having trouble sitting still
- Difficulty concentrating, remembering, or making decisions
- Thoughts of death or suicide, or suicide attempts
- Aches or pains, headaches, cramps, or digestive problems that have no clear physical cause

Bipolar Disorder (also known as Manic-Depressive Disorder). According to NIMH, bipolar disorder is "a brain disorder that causes unusual shifts in mood, energy, activity levels, and the ability to carry out day-to-day tasks." People suffering with this condition experience episodes of depression alternating with periods of mania.

There are four basic types of bipolar disorder, all of which involve demonstrable changes in mood, energy, and activity levels. These moods vacillate between periods of extreme energy and/or irritability (known as manic episodes) followed by periods of extreme sadness, hopelessness, or despair (known as depressive episodes). According to NIMH, people experiencing manic episodes may exhibit some or most of the following symptoms:

MANIC SYMPTOMS IN BIPOLAR DISORDER

- Feeling very "up," "high," or elated
- Feeling extremely energetic

- Increased activity levels
- Feeling jumpy or "wired"
- Trouble falling asleep or staying asleep
- Exhibiting pressured speech patterns, i.e., talking faster than normal
- Feeling agitated, irritable, or "touchy"
- Racing thoughts
- Attempting to do many things at once

According to NIMH, bipolar patients experiencing depressive episodes may exhibit some or most of the following symptoms:

DEPRESSIVE SYMPTOMS IN BIPOLAR DISORDER

- Feeling very sad, down, empty, or hopeless
- Having very little energy
- Exhibiting decreased activity levels
- Trouble sleeping (either too little sleep or too much)
- Feeling unable to enjoy anything
- Feeling worried and empty
- Trouble concentrating
- Forgetfulness
- Eating too much or too little
- Feeling tired or "slowed down"
- Thinking about death or suicide

OTHER COMMON MOOD DISORDERS

Persistent Depressive Disorder (also known as Dysthymia). This is a chronic, low-grade mood disorder in which symptoms of depression or irritability last for at least two years. A person diagnosed with persistent depressive disorder may experience episodes of major depression along with periods of less severe symptoms. But for a diagnosis of persistent depressive disorder, the depressive symptoms—both major symptoms and less severe ones—must last, in total, for at least two years.

Postpartum Depression: Many women feel mildly depressed or anxious after the birth of a child. These symptoms, if they occur at all, typically disappear within two weeks after delivery. Postpartum depression is a much more serious condition. Women with postpartum depression experience full-blown major depression after delivery. Feelings of extreme sadness, anxiety, and exhaustion are common, thus making it difficult for mothers to care for themselves and their babies.

Seasonal Affective Disorder (SAD): This is a form of depression that occurs during certain seasons of the year. Typically, SAD begins in the late autumn or early winter and lasts until spring or summer. Less commonly, SAD episodes may begin during the late spring or summer. Symptoms of winter seasonal affective disorder often resemble those of major depression.

THE MOST COMMON ANXIETY DISORDERS

Generalized Anxiety Disorder (GAD): This condition is characterized by chronic anxiety, by exaggerated worry, tension, and apprehension even when there is no discernable cause for those feelings.

GAD, which often begins in the teen years or early adulthood, develops slowly. According to NIMH, symptoms of GAD include the following:

- Being excessively worried about everyday things
- Having trouble controlling worries or feelings of nervousness
- Knowing that one's worries are exaggerated and excessive
- Feeling restless; having trouble relaxing
- Difficulty concentrating
- Easily startled
- Having trouble falling asleep or staying asleep
- Feeling tired most or all of the time
- Experiencing physical symptoms such as headaches, muscle aches, stomach aches, or unexplained pains
- Difficulty swallowing
- Experiencing twitches or tremors
- Being irritable or feeling "on edge"
- Sweating profusely, feeling lightheaded or out of breath

Children and teens with GAD often worry excessively about

- Performances in school, sports, or other public activities
- Catastrophes such as earthquakes or wars

Adults with GAD are often highly nervous about everyday circumstances, such as

- Job security or performance
- Health
- Finances
- The health and well-being of their children

- Being late
- Completing household chores and other responsibilities

Post-traumatic Stress Disorder (PTSD): This disorder develops in some people who have either experienced or witnessed a terrifying, life-threatening, or life-altering event. PTSD symptoms may start within one month of the traumatic event, but for many individuals, symptoms may not appear until years later. These symptoms create significant problems in social settings, work-related environments, and relationships. PTSD symptoms are generally grouped into four categories: intrusive memories, avoidance, negative changes in thinking and mood, and changes in physical and emotional reactions.

Obsessive-Compulsive Disorder (OCD): This anxiety disorder is characterized by recurrent, unwanted thoughts (obsessions) and/or repetitive behaviors (compulsions). Repetitive behaviors such as hand washing, counting, checking, or cleaning are often performed with the hope of preventing obsessive thoughts or making those thoughts go away. Performing these rituals, however, provides only temporary relief. Not performing the aforementioned repetitive behaviors causes psychological discomfort and a marked increase in anxiety.

Panic Disorder: This anxiety disorder and is characterized by unexpected and repeated episodes of intense fear (panic attacks) accompanied by physical and psychological symptoms that include:

- Sudden and repeated panic attacks that result in overwhelming feelings of anxiety and fear
- The feeling of being out of control
- The fear of death or impending doom during a panic attack

- Physical symptoms during a panic attack, such as a pounding or racing heart, sweating, chills, trembling, breathing problems, weakness or dizziness, tingly or numb hands, chest pain, stomach pain, or nausea
- An intense worry about when the next panic attack will occur
- A fear or avoidance of places where panic attacks have occurred in the past

Social Anxiety Disorder (also known as Social Phobia): This disorder is characterized by excessive self-consciousness and overwhelming anxiety resulting from social or performance situations in which the person is exposed to unfamiliar people or to possible scrutiny by others. A person with social phobia fears that he or she may act in a way—or may display anxiety-related symptoms—that will cause embarrassment or humiliation. In extreme cases, the phobia may be so broad that the sufferer experiences symptoms almost anytime he or she interacts with other people.

A Final Note

For previous generations, mental illness was often spoken about in whispers. For many sufferers and their families, emotional disorders were a source of embarrassment or shame. Thankfully, this is no longer the case. Today, mental health is a top-of-mind priority for medical professionals who are keenly aware that most mental disorders have both medical as well as psychological origins. As such, most emotional disorders are now eminently treatable. Thanks to advances in medical science, healing is available through counseling, through medication, or through a combination of the two.

If you suspect that you—or someone you care about—may be experiencing a mood disorder, an anxiety disorder, or any other psychiatric condition, don't hesitate to seek professional help. To fully experience God's abundance, you need to be spiritually and emotionally healthy. If mental health professionals can help you achieve the emotional stability you need to fully experience God's abundance here on earth, you should consider your treatment to be part of God's plan for your life.